FLIPPING HOUSES:

Buy it / Fix it/ Flip it.

Biff Sellers

TABLE OF CONTENT

INTRODUCTION

Property flipping is when an investor purchases a property below market value, make some small repairs to increase value then sell it for a large profit. Sounds simple right? It is, believe you can do it and you can. To win at this game you must be creative and think out of the box. To get what others don't have you must be what they are not. The steps are straightforward and this guide lays it all out. Take the time to research the market, pick the right property, figure out your costs, do your repairs then sell the house quickly.

In the chapters to follow we will discuss everything you need to know to get started in property flipping and real estate investing. You will learn how to research the market, find the right financing, and even how to get that house bought, fixed, and sold in no time. This can be a busy process, but expect to get better and faster with every flip. After a short period you will understand how investing works, and if you are willing to put the time and effort in, the rewards can last generations.

You've taken the first step in seeking out knowledge and rules to property flipping. House flippers choose homes that homebuyers aren't willing or able to renovate and improve them to meet buyer demand. An organized mind is key to winning this game. This book has all you need to start investing your money into real estate and seeing some of the amazing results that you can get while growing your wealth!

Once you fully understand what house flipping is and decide it's for you the world is yours, thanks again for choosing this book! Every effort has been made to ensure it is packed with useful and relevant information, please enjoy!

CHAPTER 1:

WHAT IS HOUSE FLIPPING?

House flipping is buying a home, rehabbing it into a better value then selling it. Your goal, of course, is to make a ton of money. However, flipping is not as easy and glamorous as they make it look on HGTV. It's a lot of learning, work, budgeting, and more learning. It's safe to assume that you probably know very little about house flipping and maybe even real estate in general so before you even get your loan you need to lay yourself a good solid foundation to build on. The very first thing you need to do is commit. Flipping your first house is serious and sometimes complicated business and not for the wishy-washy so you need to make sure that you are all in. If you continually educate yourself and follow the steps in this book you will set yourself up for success.

For starters, there are three main types of house flipping. Ultimately the goal of each method is to make a large profit in a short amount of time. You need to decide if you are going to buy and rehab a house to rent out or to sell. The third method is called wholesaling which is buying a house cheap, maybe slapping a coat of paint on the front, and selling it to another broker for a higher price. This is something we get into a little later in the book and is usually reserved for seasoned flippers.

3

What you do with your flip is also called your exit strategy. Keep in mind that real estate comes with a fair amount of risk. Market depreciation, time of the year, economic flux, and many more risks are always looming but with rigor, planning and organization you will hopefully avoid them.

Deciding if you want to rent or sell will determine a lot of things. For example, if you are going to rent your property out then you only need to rehab it to functional, clean level. If you are planning on selling it right away, you will have to spend a lot more time and money on the renovations. Let me break down the pros and cons of each method.

Finding the Right House to Flip

Beginners spend a lot of time wondering and worrying whether they have found the right house to make a profitable flip or not. Let's put your mind to rest! Any place that meets the numbers criteria is the right house. It doesn't have to be in the perfect neighborhood, have excellent curb appeal, need minimal repairs, or be a home that you love. One thing it MUST have is motivated sellers; because you're going to ask them to accept a significant discount to get them out of their house.

Apply Your Flipping Formula

In most markets, there is a shortage of homes that will work for flipping. That's why investors are always willing to pay for leads that turn into a successful sale, but we'll talk about working that angle a little later. The only thing prohibiting you from finding houses that might qualify to flip is your imagination. How creative can you be when it comes to locating a home that qualifies? Forget for a moment whether the seller is motivated; we'll discuss that later. All we're concerned about right now is finding homes that might work with your flipping formula, and here's what we mean by that.

Before you consider approaching the seller to negotiate a price, you need to know your bottom line. Every house is different because of its market value and the cost of repairs. You need to know the answer to these three questions to crunch the numbers successfully.

1. What is the current market value of the home?
2. What are the costs of the estimated repairs?
3. What will be the value of the home after all the repairs?

That doesn't sound too hard, right? Wrong! The answers to these questions will require a great deal of research, questioning, and negotiations. To give you a better idea of just how complicated it can be to get the answers to these three little questions, let's break them down into steps.

Step #1—Setting the Current Market Value

- Once you have located a home that peaks your interest, contact real estate agent or do an internet search to find homes that have sold in that neighborhood. If possible, go no further back than the past six months. Also, try to stay within a few blocks radius of the house you intend to flip. If you need to expand your search area, go out no further than one mile. In a perfect world, you should be able to find several houses that have sold in the past two to five months within the area.

- Websites like Zillow or Trulia should give a good description of the house. As you make your comparisons with the house, you are interested in flipping and the ones that have sold; the following items will need to be reviewed. Some of the information will require some digging. You might need to search public records. If the house was listed, you could find out who listed it and contact the listing agent. They are usually quite helpful in providing information. When it becomes too difficult to find what you need, you will need to contact a court clerk's office or a realtor for help. When you do, the realtor needs to be compensated. Paying commissions can put a hitch in your negotiations since part of the way to talk the sellers into discounting their homes is because they won't have to pay commissions. Some brokerages specialize in working with investors. Finding them will be a time- and a money-saving asset to your company.

- Sales Price
- Financing (Terms)
- Number of bedrooms
- Number of baths
- Square Footage
- Lot Size
- Swimming Pool
- Air Conditioning/Heating
- Two or Three Car Garage/or Driveway
- Year Built
- Roof Type
- What Type of Sale (Foreclosure, Divorce, etc.)
- Fencing
- Type of Home (2-Story; Condo; Single-Family, etc.)
- Landscaping
- Overall Condition

Once you have compared properties in the area that have sold, you can set the current market value of the home you want to flip. It may be necessary to drive by the property to get a better idea of how your house compares with the others that have sold. You can even pay the homeowners a visit and let them know that you are interested in a home in the neighborhood and would like to ask them a few questions. New owners are usually proud of their purchase and more than willing to answer a few questions.

Having a good relationship with your title agent and company is also important. In many cases, they will have access to information that you don't. They can save you a lot of time and supply you with current and accurate information.

Step #2—Figuring the Costs of Estimated Repairs

Estimating costs might be tough because some issues will be hidden and pop up later as ugly surprises. During your initial inspection of the home, you'll need to look for the following.

- Landscaping
- Roof Condition
- Exterior Paint or Siding
- Wood Trim/Eaves/Gutters
- Windows
- Front/Back Doors
- Garage Door(s)
- Sidewalk/Driveway/Walkways
- Fuse Box
- Electric Meter (Has it been tagged for non-payment?)
- Trash on Grounds or Inside Garage/House
- Lots of Stuff Left Behind (Additional Hauling Cost)
- Flooring Condition
- Wall Repairs
- Foundation Issues
- Doors/Molding/Trim in Need of Repairs

- Hot Water Heater
- Year of Air Conditioning Unit/Heating Unit
- Light Fixtures that Need Repair or Replacement
- Attractive Layout/Awkward Floor plan
- Kitchen Appliances/Cabinets/Countertops/Sink
- Electrical Outlets
- Bathroom Shower/Tubs/Sinks
- Pool/Pump/Cool Decking/Patio Cover/Pool House

Note: *Take lots of pictures inside and out to show your construction people.*

Getting estimates and feedback from your construction people is critical, especially for beginner flippers. After you've been in the business for a while, you get good at eyeballing things, but at first, you'll want to rely on the professionals to give you accurate figures.

Step #3—Figuring the Value of the Home after Refurbishing

Using the same area as you did when finding the current market value, look at the homes that are for sale. Find out what they are selling for, and compare them with the home you are flipping. In a perfect world, after the repairs are made, and the house looks incredible, how does yours compare with the others? Knowing what other homes are selling for will not increase the real value of your flip, but it will let you know what buyers will see as they shop for a new home. If you were a buyer, which home would you prefer to purchase, and why? This is particularly the case for upper-end homes, because your customers are somewhat limited and you'll be vying for the same people.

Let's look at a sample formula, shall we?
Current Market Value of the Flip$100,000
Cost of repairs$ 25,000
Value after Repairs$170,000

Formula: Take the current market value of $100,000 times 70 percent, which equals $70,000. You base everything off only 70 percent of the current market value. That is where you build your profit margins. Now subtract the cost of your repairs, which is $25,000. You are then at $50.000. If you want to make a reasonable profit from the house, you should not offer more than $50,000.

I can hear you now justifying an adjustment in the offering price of $50,000. Don't think your profit in the house will be $120,000 and consider offering more money to the sellers. Here's why! There are many more costs that might not be evident in the beginning. Here are additional funds that might need to be spent to sell the home.

- Unexpected repairs
- Realtor Commissions
- Attorney Fees

- House Payments if the Home isn't Quickly Flipped
- Marketing/Advertising Cost

You also need to subtract your costs for doing business, like car maintenance and gas, office equipment, professional associations and club memberships, and any licenses. With some homes, you will enjoy more profits, and with others, you'll be pulling your hair out to make sure you break even. So, some of that additional money collected in profits from one home might have to be used to offset another.

Where Do You Find the Houses to Flip?

There are a variety of ways to hunt for and locate potential flip houses. One is to go directly to the sellers. I'm sure you've seen those signs on the road that say "I'll buy your house for cash?" That's from an investor who is most likely using that 70 percent principle. Sellers who call on those signs are usually very motivated to sell their home and willing to entertain the offer.

Another way to find houses to flip is to advertise in the newspaper or online. Create a website and promote your services. Work on social media and LinkedIn. I've heard of investors going to the Real Estate Investors Meetings or contacting "For Rent" owners to see if they might be ready to get rid of the rental and sell. Some new investors just drive through neighborhoods where they would like to rehab a house and think it would turn over quickly. Another place to look for homes is in public court, documents for recent divorcees who may need to sell quickly. Or, attend county tax sales, auctions, and foreclosures where you can pick up property inexpensively.

Keep in mind; you need to have your method of funding in order when you are ready to purchase. What is motivating the seller to give you a huge discount is that you have the money and you can close right away.

Why Would People Take a Big Hit on Their Houses?

It's impossible to say why some people are willing to take such a deep discount on their homes. It could be that a family member died who owned the house, and they just want to divest themselves of the responsibility and collect the cash. It could be the sellers have lost their job or just got a divorce and cannot afford the house any longer, but they don't want it to hurt their credit. Some people have not kept up with needed repairs on the house, and now they can't afford to do everything, so they're willing to sell at a low price. Then, there are those who just don't want to hassle with the process of a traditional sale, and so they sell quick, at a discount, and move on with life.

The bottom line is, do you care why they are selling if they agree to your price and terms? I don't think so! Pick the house, crunch the numbers, and if it works, make your move. One of the worse things beginner investors do is get emotionally involved with the house they are flipping. Don't get attached. It's not about how beautiful the house is or how much you love the neighborhood unless you want to live there.

The difference between buying a home to live in and buying one you're going to flip is your emotional involvement. Regular buyers make their decision emotionally and justify the purchase logically. You, as an investor, do just the opposite. You buy logically but appeal to the sellers' emotions to get the lowest price possible. The lower the price, the greater your profits. There's no need to feel sorry for the sellers, even if they take less money than they wanted. Emotions and feelings in this situation is like oil and water (Non Mixing). This is business and everybody wins and looses. Selling to you is a hassle-free way to dump what they considered to be a liability. They'll be relieved to be rid of the house and get on with their lives.

If you think you've found a great house to flip, but you just can't make yourself pull the trigger, there are some ways to build your business that doesn't require much money or risks. Here are a few ways that might help you ease your way into house flipping.

Work for a Finder's Fee

If you have located a house that has potential as a flip but you don't want to take the chance, or you have no funds, then call some investors and work for a finder's fee. You'll become a part of their team for a while and find some great opportunities for them to flip. Be sure to sign an agreement with them that they'll pay you a finder's fee for the homes you give them that end in a successfully executed agreement.

The amount investors are willing to pay usually range from $500 on up to a couple of thousand dollars, depending on the profitability potential in the house. No money comes out of your pocket; you just act as the middle man. It can be very labor intensive for an investor to locate houses, so you and your company can be a real asset to them.

Lastly, be sure to stash some of that money to prepare you for the time you will be doing the refurbishing. After several of these types of transactions, you'll have a tidy little sum to enable you to flip fearlessly. It's amazing what a little nest egg will do to combat your fears of flipping. You don't have to be richer than other investors to clinch the deal; you need to be smarter. And you're getting smarter by the moment, don't you think?

CHAPTER 2:

REAL ESTATE PROPERTIES

Residential Real Estate

The properties under this category involve apartments and homes for residential use by families and individuals. Some of the properties in this category include a built-in service business element such as assisted living facilities for the elderly, or luxury apartments with all services available for residents.

Rental leases for such properties run for about six months to one year, depending on the needs of the tenants and the owners. These short-term leases make residential real estate easily adaptable to various market conditions, considering that you can make changes every time the lease comes up for renewal. You can read more about this in a separate chapter dedicated to this aspect.

Commercial Real Estate

Consisting largely of office buildings, the leases for commercial real estate can be locked in for a long period of time, unlike residential real estate. However, having long-term leases can be a double-edged sword. The good thing is that if you get long-term tenants who agree to a high rent, then your cash flow is going to be unchanged, irrespective of downfalls in the outside market conditions.

Contrarily, the reverse is also true. If you have locked yourself into a long-term lease, then you will not be able to benefit from upward trends, if any, taking place in the outside market conditions. You can read more about this in a separate chapter dedicated to this aspect.

Industrial Real Estate

The properties under this category include distribution centers, warehouses, factories and other manufacturing facilities, assembly plants, storage units, etc. The leases for such real estate will usually be long-term and will come with similar double-edged sword conditions, such as commercial real estate.

Retail Real Estate

As a retail real estate investor, you will own properties in the form of strip malls, conventional malls, and huge shopping malls. Your tenants may include hair salons, retail shops, restaurants, and others. It is possible to include a percentage of the sales into the rent too, in some cases. The percentage of sales as payment can be an incentive for the landlord to do his or her bit to attract more shoppers to the retail property.

Mixed-Use Real Estate

In this kind of property, the investor has a stake in both rental and commercial real estate. Typical examples of such properties are apartment complexes in which the ground is dedicated to retail real estate, such as shops, restaurants, etc.; the next couple of floors are given over to office space; and the floors above these are residential apartments.

In addition to the above, there are other unconventional methods of getting into real estate such as leasing a property (thereby reducing the need for large capital) and then subleasing parts of it to other tenants. You can also invest in mezzanine securities, which lend money to real estate projects. If the money you invested is not returned (with said profits) for any reason, these mezzanine securities allow you to secure equity ownership.

Yes, there are esoteric ways of getting into real estate investing. But, the average real estate investor looks to conventional home or building ownership options, especially if it is the first time for the individual. So, let us look at this in a little more detail.

Single Family Homes

Investing in single-family homes in many U.S. markets is a hot market to get into. Over the last three years, 30% of the single family homes purchased have been used as rental properties. (Sullivan, 2017). Investing in a single family home and turning it into a rental is the next type of property to invest in.

A Single Family Home is a detached, stand-alone house. The investor owns the home and the land it is on. Some single family homes are part of a Planned Unit Development (PUD). This is a community made up of single family homes or townhomes. (Agranoff, 2012) There is an HOA and fees are paid monthly, quarterly, or annually. The fees cover the community roads or buildings that are part of the common area of the community. Some developments have play areas for kids and a community swimming pool.

Single-family homes are popular rentals and sought out by the public for a number of reasons. People will always need a place to call home, and will look for a property that fits their needs, and has a rent that is affordable. That being said, single-family homes are in high demand. Families with two to three children (and sometimes more) usually look for 3 bedrooms, 2 bathrooms home to rent. A family presents the possibility of their renting long-term while the children attend schools in the area and participate in community and school events.

Another attraction of single-family homes that attract renters is the ability for tenants to have pets. Townhomes and condominiums allow pets, but many of them insist on a size cut-off for dogs. This means that a dog cannot weigh or be larger than the parameters set by the HOA. Some HOAs even restrict the number of pets a tenant can have, and certain breeds also fall under restrictions. A single-family home affords that a tenant can own a pet, and unless there is a size restriction stated in the lease, can own a dog without limitations.

Pets are covered by fees that are due at the beginning of a lease. If there is normal wear and tear to the property, and there is no damage caused by a pet, the fee can be made refundable at the end of the lease.

Properties that can be continuous rentals in college towns are another option for an investor to a profitable investment. College students who want to live off campus look for rental properties where a few people can split the rent. An off-campus residence is less cramped and confining than a dorm room to live in, making renting a house an attractive option.

Investors renting their property to any tenant should be very specific in the wording of the lease. In order to protect their investment, a lease usually should have stringent rules to abide by. Loud parties, noise, additional tenants who are not on the lease, causing disruption in the neighborhood, or damage to the property that is not normal wear and tear can be stipulated as a breach of the lease.

Townhouse and Condominiums

A townhouse and a condominium are the next types of real estate properties that an investor can invest in for rentals. There are differences between the two. Let's look at what they are.

Townhouse

A Townhouse is a style of construction. It is like a single family house, where the investor owns both the building and the land, but the difference between them is that a townhouse is not free standing and separate. There is ownership of the front and backyard, but it attached, sharing a common wall with to the next townhouse. Townhouses are usually built in a row and commonly are two stories, and don't have neighbors above or below the structure. A townhome can be a style of a condominium. (Agranoff, 2012) A townhouse can also be part of a PUD, with HOA dues used for upkeep of the community and community amenities.

Condominium

A Condominium (Condo) is where you and other members of the HOA jointly own the actual structure of the building, the common areas such as swimming pool, tennis courts, and any other amenities in the complex. The airspace and the interior of the structure are owned individually, but the building is not owned individually by any of the owners. (Agranoff, 2012)

There are a number of different structure styles that can be considered condominiums. A condo can be a ranch style attached units, 2 or 3 story units, or they can be an apartment style in a building. They can be one or two floors and can have a basement. Dependent on the configuration of the structure, there can be a neighbor above or below, or both.

When you own a condo, you do not own the land that the structure is on. A condo owner only owns the unit. It is taxed as an individual unit and sometimes a percentage of the common areas. Ownership of either a townhouse or a condominium refers to the type of ownership, not type of structure. (Agranoff, 2012)

Investing in a townhouse or condominium as a rental property comes with a number of rules and regulations. Covenants, Conditions, and Restrictions (CC&Rs) and HOA Bylaws.

The CC&Rs cover regulations on what can and cannot be done in a planned community. They are the rules of the neighborhood. Examples of what some of these are can be the following: (Loftsgordon)

- Garbage cans must be pulled off the street after trash pickup
- Cars must be parked at the curb
- Adults must accompany children to the swimming pool

HOA Bylaws are established by the Association to manage the Planned Unit Development (PUD). They are usually set up as a non-profit corporation. As a corporation, they have a Board of Directors with a President, Vice-President, Treasurer, and

Secretary. It governs the business of the HOA. Some of the duties of the Board deal with HOA meetings and events. (Loftsgordon)

- How meetings are managed
- Duties of the officers of the Board
- Membership voting rights
- How many meetings the HOA will have over the year

Investing in a PUD or a condominium can present limitations for an investor. As stated before, there are limitations as to how many rental properties are allowed. Before investing, become familiar with the Association bylaws to check if the community has already reached the percentage level allowed for rentals.

Another aspect to consider is the HOA dues. Paying HOA dues are an owner's responsibility. Depending on the development, these dues can be high. The market value of rent that can be charged to a tenant may be diminished by the due's fees.

There are also special assessments to consider. A special assessment may be charged to the owners for a service that is not covered by the usual dues. Fees are shared proportionately based on the percentage of property owned. If an HOA has a healthy reserve account, it is possible that special assessments can be covered by the reserve. (Venzon)

Investigate what types of reserves are on hand. Speak to other owners to find out how the Association handles the reserve funds. Check the age and condition of the development. If it's an older development, there may be excessive repairs that need to be made and reserves may not cover them. Has the development met the quota of rental properties allowed? They may have and investing in a property that can't be rented is not how it will be profitable. (Venzon)

All of these points just covered will help an investor to decide whether or not investments in these types of real estate are worth it.

Investing in a below market value real estate property that can be rented relatively quickly after repairs and code inspections are passed, can be a sound and profitable investment. When the property is ready and goes on the market, the phone will start ringing with eager applicants. Proper screening of prospective tenants, a continuous cash flow, and all the other benefits attached to investing in rental properties, will make for profits an investor will want to repeat again and again.

Foreclosure?

Foreclosure typically involves a lawsuit to which a bank, mortgage lender, or other creditor seeks to take a property back that was secured for a debt. The bank or lender can take the property back or request that the property is sold to pay off the debt.

Important Key Terms

Default— a mortgage is considered in default when more than one payment is due and is unpaid. The mortgage is generally due on the 1st of each month. Most banks allow a 15-day grace period.

Delinquent Payment— a mortgage payment that is not made by the day it is due.

Equity— The value of the property deducted from what you still owed on the property.

Forbearance— Typically a written or oral agreement to repay the delinquency of a loan over a period of time.

Important Tips

Federally insured mortgages, such as FHA, HUD, or VA, are granted special rights under foreclosure protection. FHA, HUD, or VA mortgages may extend the period before foreclosure, award moderate repayment plans or even allow for the government agency to buy out the lender.

You will need to contact the mortgage lender to find out what options are available if you have a federally insured mortgage.

It is very helpful to understand that foreclosure processes and laws vary from state to state.

Judicial Foreclosure

Explaining lis pendens: Filed by a lender, a lis pendens is the formal notice that starts the foreclosure process in a judicial foreclosure state.

Non-judicial Foreclosure

Non-judicial foreclosures are started with a deed of trust that contains a power of sale clause. The clause facilitates the trustee to initiate a mortgage foreclosure sale, without ever having to go to court. The trustee is required to issue a notice of default and notify the homeowner. If the homeowner does not respond, the trustee may then initiate a foreclosure sale.

CHAPTER 3:

THE TAX ANGLE

A tax lien sale is the sale, conducted by a governmental agency, of tax liens for delinquent taxes on real estate. It is one of two methodologies used by governmental agencies to collect delinquent taxes owed on real estate, the other being the tax deed sale.

I. Sale process

In a tax lien sale, the lien (for delinquent taxes, accrued interest, and costs associated with the sale) is offered to prospective investors at public auction. Traditionally, auctions were held in person; however, Internet-based auctions (especially within large counties having numerous liens) have grown in popularity as this method allows for bidders from outside the area to participate.

In the event that more than one investor seeks the same lien, depending on state law the winner will be determined by one of five methods:

Bid Down the Interest. Under this method, the stated rate of return offered by the government is the maximum rate of return allowed. However, investors can accept lower rates of return, including zero percent in some cases (though this is rare in practice). The investor accepting the lowest rate of return is the winner. In the event more than one investor will accept the same lower rate, a random or rotational method (see below) will be used to break ties. (Florida and Arizona use this method)

Premium. Under this method, the investor willing to pay the highest "premium" (or excess above the lien amount) will be the winner. The premium may or may not earn interest, and may or may not be paid back to the investor upon redemption of the lien. (Colorado uses this method)

Random Selection. Under this method, a bidder will be randomly selected from those offering a bid. Usually a computer is used to make the selection, but in smaller jurisdictions more rudimentary methods may be used. Nevada uses Random selection since it is supposed to be the first buyer but it is hard to determine who was the first person to the sale.

Rotational Selection. Under this method, the first lien offered for sale will be offered to the investor holding bidder number one, who has the right of first refusal. If bidder number one refuses the lien, bidder number two may then bid. However, bidder number one will not be offered another lien until his number comes up again in the rotation. The next lien will go to the next number in line. Under this method, the investor has virtually no control over which liens s/he will obtain in the bidding, except to take or refuse what is offered.

Bid Down the Ownership. Used in Iowa and few other states, the investor willing to purchase the lien for the lowest percent of encumbrance on the property will be awarded the lien. For example, a bidder may agree to take a lien on only 95% of the property. If the lien is not redeemed, the investor would only receive 95% ownership of the property with the remaining 5% owned by the original owner. In practice, few investors will bid on liens for less than full right to the property or sale proceeds. Therefore, with multiple owners bidding on 100% encumbrance, the process then generally reverts to the random selection.

Liens not sold at auction are considered "struck" (or sold) to the entity (usually the county) conducting the auction. Some states allow "over the counter" purchases of liens not sold at auction.

II. Redemption process

The investor must wait a specified period of time (referred to as the "redemption period"), during which time the lien (plus interest and any other fees) may be repaid. Usually the lien holder is not permitted during this period to contact the property owner (or anyone else having an interest in the property, such as the mortgage holder) to demand payment or threaten foreclosure, or else the certificate can be forfeit.

In some jurisdictions, the lien holder must agree to pay subsequent unpaid property taxes during the redemption period in order to protect his/her interest. If the lien holder does not pay such taxes, a subsequent lien holder would "buy out" the prior lien holder's interest.

Once the redemption period is over, the lien holder may initiate foreclosure proceedings. The proceedings (the costs of which must be paid by the lien holder, though a redeeming property owner may be required to pay them as part of redemption) may result in either acquiring title to the property (normally this will be in the form of a quitclaim deed) or a tax deed sale of the property where the lien holder has the right of first bid (and may participate by making additional bids if s/he so chooses).

In Illinois a "Tax Deed" delivers a clean title as the court removes all clouds on title in the order directing the issuance of the deed. During the period between the initiation of proceedings and actual foreclosure, the property owner still has the opportunity to repay the lien with interest plus the costs incurred to foreclose.

If the lienholder does not act within a specified period of time, as defined by state law, the lien is forfeited and the holder loses his investment. This period of time ranges anywhere from 7 to 10 years and cannot be extended unless the tax lien is officially in the process of a tax deed application of Judicial Foreclosure.

A lien issued in error of state law is repaid, but usually at a far lower interest rate than had the lien been valid.

III. Benefits of tax lien investing

The maximum rate of return on a tax lien can be far higher than other investments. For example, Florida offers a maximum rate of 18% (1.5% per month, with a guaranteed 5% return regardless of time held), while Arizona offers a maximum rate of 16%. Iowa offers a guaranteed 2% per month (or 24% annual return).

IV. Pitfalls of tax lien investing

Payment is usually required at purchase or within a very short time afterward (often no more than 24–72 hours). Failure to pay the full amount results in all lien certificates purchased by the investor being cancelled, and may result in the investor losing his/her deposit and/or being barred from future sales.

In many states, further actions must be taken to protect the lien holder's rights after purchase of a lien, and generally within a certain period of time; failure to comply exactly with such requirements may make the lien worthless.

In "bid down the interest" jurisdictions, valuable properties are usually bid to the lowest rate possible greater than zero percent. (For example, Florida permits the interest rate to be bid down to a minuscule 0.25% – though it guarantees a minimum 5% return – while Arizona allows the bid to be as low as 1%.)

Similarly, in "premium" states, valuable properties are bid up above the means of an average investor.

Unlike a certificate of deposit, tax liens are illiquid. They cannot be "cashed in" (resold to the taxing authority), but must be held until either they are repaid or the holder takes action to foreclose. (It is possible, however, to assign one's interest in a tax lien to another party.)

Tax Lien properties sold in non-Judicial Foreclosure states are conveyed to the highest bidder via a tax deed. The holder of the tax deed would then have to file a quiet title action, in the county where the property is situated, to clear of title defects. Although properties sold on tax deeds can be transferred, all financial institutions require a marketable title on property they will be financing.

Tax Liens that you hold on properties may become worthless due to municipal liens and assessments on the property. These liens and assessments (and their related interest) can increase the monies owed to a point that the property is deemed worthless.

2. ALL ABOUT TAX DEED SALES

A tax deed sale is the forced sale, conducted by a governmental agency, of real estate for nonpayment of taxes. It is one of two methodologies used by governmental agencies to collect delinquent taxes owed on real estate, the other being the tax lien sale.

Tax deed sale process

Real estate taxes are considered delinquent if not paid within a specified period of time. If the taxes are not paid, after legal requirements are met (such as giving proper notice to the property owner as well as others holding an interest in the property, or by filing required action in the courts), the property is offered for sale at a public auction.

At the sale, the minimum bid is generally the amount of back taxes owed plus interest, as well as costs associated with selling the property. In the event the property is not purchased, title may revert to the governmental entity that offered the property for sale. Title is generally transferred in a tax deed sale through a form of limited warranty or quitclaim deed (sometimes styled as Tax Deed or Sheriff's Deed); the purchaser would most likely then need to initiate a quiet title action in order to resell the property later (as a quitclaim deed is generally insufficient to acquire title insurance). However, the property can be sold from one investor to another by cash or owner financing using a limited warranty, Sheriff's Deed, or even a quitclaim deed.

Some jurisdictions allow for a post-sale "redemption period," whereby the former owner has a specified amount of time to reclaim the property by repaying the amount bid at auction plus a penalty. For example, Texas allows a 6-month (for non-homestead, non-agricultural properties) or two-year period (homestead or agricultural properties), with a flat 25% penalty to be added to the amount paid at the sale (50% after the first year), while Tennessee allows a full year, with a 10% penalty. As such, purchasers of properties at tax deed sales are cautioned not to make major improvements on the property until after the redemption period has expired.

A tax deed sale may also be used in conjunction with a tax lien, whereby the lienholder (instead of a governmental agency) starts the process toward forcing a public sale of the property. In those instances the lienholder's investment (the price of the lien plus any additional costs necessary to start the tax deed sale process, such as required fees and payment of any still-unpaid taxes or buyout of other certificate holders' interests) constitutes the minimum bid;

if no other bids are received at the sale then the lienholder will take title to the property subject to redemption periods (if applicable) or any lawsuit to overturn the sale (for example, failure to provide proper notice).

CHAPTER 4:

THINGS TO AVOID

Flipping houses can be quite lucrative, once an investor begins to win there are common pitfalls they must look out for. Being aware of these five most common mistakes can help you not to turn the flip into a flop. Many experienced investors have made these mistakes. The costs were so great that it almost put them out of business after their first flip. So, take the advice of seasoned flippers and make sure you aren't making these common mistakes.

1. Over Improve the House for the Neighborhood

Most flippers began their business because they want to make money, and they love to turn a beat-up, run-down house into a beautiful home. While it's important to love your work, you don't want to over-improve the house for the neighborhood. Keep the area and targeted buyer in mind when you are making improvements. Could you install more expensive and higher quality flooring that would cause the home to look better and be more desirable? Sure, but would that extra cost eat into your pocketbook and price the house out of the market? It could!

The best way to prevent the temptation of over-improving the house is to set an amount you'll pay for each repair and refuse to go over that amount. If you have budgeted $4,000 for flooring, then stay within your number. It's amazing how a little here and a little there can bust your budget. Add all those "littles" up, and they can turn into one big loss.

The whole idea isn't to have the most expensive house on the block. You're not in the business of Hollywood flipping; it's reality. The goal is to make as much profit as you can, and that means sticking to your original plan. When you shop-do so reasonably. You're not going to live in the house. You want it to look good, be clean and fresh, and attract your target market. Avoid putting million dollar amenities into a $100,000 home.

2. Want to Make All Your Profit on One Flip

The key to consistent flipping success is to flip many medium-priced houses and make a reasonable profit on all of them. Many beginners in the business try to make all their money in one flip, so they go out and buy an expensive house, sink a ton of money in repairs, and end up having it eat into their profits because they need to hold onto it longer than expected. Buying and flipping expensive homes doesn't necessarily mean you'll make more money. What it does mean is that you risk more money to "perhaps" make more profits—perhaps being the operative word.

Take your profits in small bites. Flip several smaller homes and make your profits $20,000 to $25,000 on each. It will be easier on your wallet as well as your well-being. There's so much less stress when you have less to lose. Besides, your buyers' pool is larger for medium-priced homes, and you'll be able to flip them quicker. Your repairs are usually less costly as well. Get some practice flipping smaller homes before you play with the big boy flippers.

Think about it, what's better—to flip one large home and turn a $60,000 profit or flip five smaller homes and make $125,000 profit? You learn more about flipping houses by doing more, so flipping five houses would give you greater benefits and experience than one larger, more expensive one.

3. Don't Have Time to Manage the Flip Properly

Poor management happens when newbies try to flip houses while they continue to work a full-time job. It's possible to flip and work at the same time if you are willing to build your business slower and you are patient with the work. You won't make as much money, but it's a way to keep your sanity and financial freedom. If you do have to work another full-time job while you begin building your house flipping business, don't try to do all the work yourself. The frustration and time spent will probably prove your downfall. Hire a good team of experts to do the job and someone to manage the flip while you work your other job.

Some new flippers try to work and refurbish their flips on the weekends. Then what could have been a labor of love turns into just more "honey do" weekends. Soon you find that you don't want to go out to the site, and the work just doesn't get done. Fruitful and timely flipping takes someone to keep a constant eye on the progress. Because time is money when flipping, every moment wasted because you are tired eats into your bottom line.

Not only is time wasted, but it's difficult to watch over your construction crew and oversee quality craftsmanship if you're never there. If you want to continue your day job while flipping, you ought to consider getting a partner who can manage the flips on a full-time basis. Having a 50/50 partner doesn't mean your profits will be cut in half as well. If a responsible and reliable partner allows you to flip quicker for higher profits, and flip more houses in a shorter period, then you might make up a lot of the money in the long run.

4. Begin Flipping with Little Knowledge and Even Less Skill

Hopefully, this won't be you because by reading this book you already show an interest in gaining experience before jumping into the business of flipping houses. Congratulations! You are one step ahead of many one-time, would-be flippers. However, don't let this book be your one and only. Keep reading and attending seminars and investor meetings. Find several mentors who are willing to share their experiences and knowledge.

With every business comes competition, but don't think of competition as being a negative impact on your ability to grow and build your business. Competition makes you sharp and encourages you to keep up-to-date with the market. Find out what's trendy to do for repairs and how you can save money on furnishings. Discover what buyers are asking for, and add those things to your flips. Investigate what types of homes are easier to sell, and buy them. Don't wait for the market to change you, be proactive and stay ahead of the pack.

Take every opportunity to learn new skills that will enable you to save money on the next flip. Watch your skilled laborers, and pay attention to their cost-cutting secrets. Preview homes and see what makes one house attract buyers while another home of the same value sits on the market. Notice some repairs aren't going to increase the value of the home, but they will give your flips that "WOW" factor that catches the eyes of realtors® and their buyers. In a way, these strategies will increase profits because they'll help you to sell the house quicker.

5. Going too far from the path

Not sticking to your original plan is the number one mistake flippers make. It's not that they don't know the highest price they can pay and still make a profit; it's usually moving into more expensive repairs that get new flippers into trouble. They budgeted one number and then begin to compromise their budget on several items. Before you know it, your numbers are upside down, and you're stuck with a house you can't sell for the price you want.

You just cannot compromise on the math. Commit yourself to making zero adjustments to what you think you can get for the house after the repairs. It's a dangerous game you play when you begin to justify putting more expensive repairs into a home in hopes of getting more for it when you sell.

Most of these mistakes occur because you've let yourself become too emotionally involved with the home. Let's face it; we're conditioned to feel warm and fuzzy about homes. Home is where the heart is; it's where our fondest childhood memories live. Most of us tend to associate homes with happiness, security, and safety. It's easy to see why the temptation is there to make your flip the best in the neighborhood. However, thinking of your flip as you do your personal family home will block your ability to make the proper improvements and generate the most profits.

We can't say this enough-- IT'S A BUSINESS! Get your head in and your heart out. You've heard entrepreneurs say that they put their heart and soul into their business to make it grow. Well, we're telling you to put your business head and logical reasoning into your business and leave your emotions outside.

Don't purchase a flip because you fall in love with the house. Don't pick products because they're what you'd want in your home. Make decisions based on what will give you the greatest profits in the shortest timeframe.

The biggest mistake is letting fear keep you from flipping. Some people are fascinated with the prospect of flipping houses, and they learn about it and dream about doing it but never move forward. What a shame to let fear keep you from success. Knowledge and experience are the best ways to battle your fears. You're right to fear the risks. Flipping houses does entail taking chances. If it were so easy, you'd be spending all your time fighting off the competition. Everybody would be flipping houses.

While we're facing things, it's time for you to realize that flipping houses for real aren't like it is on television. You don't always turn the house in a couple of months. You don't always get a contract the first day you hold the house open. And, sad to say, you won't always make a huge profit. With some, you keep your fingers crossed in hopes of breaking even. And, you won't be wearing your Sunday best to clean up the flip. You'll be cleaning a lot of other people's filth, and there will be many mysterious pests hiding just beneath the surface of EVERYTHING! One of the fears you will most have to battle is the fear of unwanted residents. Ask any investor; they love to share their horror stories with flips. You may find unwelcome squatters residing in a back bedroom, bugs, dead animals, the remnants of teenage parties, and all sorts of previous leftovers. Don't worry, though; you'll be prepared for the worst ahead of time. You can always smell the problems before you see them.

Okay, if you've read all this and still want to flip houses, you're ready for the next step. When you pocket $25,000 to $50,000 on a refurbish, it makes everything worth it.

CHAPTER 5:

MASTERS MIND STATE

Real Transformation Through Renovation

You finally managed to get your hands-on that sweet ownership title - congratulations are in order! But before you celebrate your success, keep in mind that the battle has only just begun. Oh, humble flipper - there's a whole lot left to do if you want to turn that title into profit, and it starts with your renovation.

Renovating an old home restores value because it makes the property livable and aesthetically appealing. After all - no one could ever see themselves living in a run-down shack! Buyers gravitate towards fresh coats of paint and clean new tiles, so it's important to make those changes if you want to reel in buyers without having to push such a hard sell.

Just like the home selection process, there are a few guidelines you should keep in mind when planning out a renovation. These key points should help direct you towards making the right choices, so you get the best returns out of your effort without having to spend more than you're willing to or capable of.

The Foundations of a Cost-Effective Renovation

Understanding what is needed and what is considered a luxury will help set boundaries and keep your budget out of the red. As a general rule, you'll want to do the least without sacrificing build quality and aesthetic. This will help keep your project within reasonable cost and time limits without affecting its appeal to your prospective buyers.

Keep in Line with Competition

You probably thought that the first step to planning a renovation is doing a thorough inspection of your property. But on the contrary, the first step is actually scoping other similar properties for sale in your area. Sound funny? It definitely does, but there's a completely valid explanation.

Consider this scenario: you just got your hands-on a 3BR/2TB 1500 square foot home in a quiet suburban locality. Without stopping to check the competition, you order an extensive renovation.

You're thinking of painting it a new exterior color, landscaping with new trees and bushes to line the perimeter walls, switching out the wooden floorboards with marble tiles, remodeling the stairs, and giving the bathrooms completely new fixtures, tubs, and toilets.

It would cost you roughly $65,000 to get everything done. You call your contractor, tell them to get started, and watch the project unfold over 5 months. When it's all done, you have a fully renovated house that looks like a pretty picture ripped out of a magazine. Now, it's time to lie and wait for those hungry house hunters to snap up your listing.

Unfortunately, things don't really turn out how you had expected. It's been 4 months since listing, and you notice that there hasn't been a lot of activity. What's the problem?

Upon inspecting nearby listings of a similar size, you find that they're far cheaper. With the same 3BR/2TB provision and 1500 square foot land area, these houses are modest, yet clean and livable. They look decent and have a rustic charm with their wooden floorings and accents.

These houses have gotten quite a few bids over the course of your renovation. And what was originally 4 properties are now just 2 - with the other 2 having been sold since you purchased your home. Yikes.

Unfortunately for you, the cost you spent on the renovations will make it impossible to cut your selling price back unless you're willing to make just break even. If you do manage to push the numbers back a little, you might just have a few thousands left behind after you pay all the fees and taxes once you make your sale.

So, sadly this flip n' fix might be a bit of flop. The pitfall? Not checking the competition. The purpose of familiarizing yourself with other available listings of similar qualities in your locality is to help establish the aesthetic and quality that buyers will see in the area.

If your home looks worse, then buyers might be more inclined to purchase slightly more expensive houses to avoid the need to make any changes on their own. If your home is too renovated, then you might have spent too much to get your property to look way different while weighing down its cost. Sure, it looks wonderful - but with a far smaller budget, prospective purchasers can get really decent properties in the same area that are just as livable.

Essentially, what you want is to look even just slightly better than competition. You don't need to pay for such expensive changes that make you exceptionally different - all you need to aim for is cleaner and fresher! In a lot of cases, that could mean just allowing a few cosmetic changes to give your house that brand-new look and feel.

In Smitty Longwood's words - "I've seen gold-plated taps worth $6,000 USD each, or you can have the same water coming out of a perfectly nice-looking $60 USD tap. It's easy to get carried away." Don't let the desire to create America's next most iconic home sway you from your purpose - do the least but be the best.

Know When to DIY

We're not all home improvement experts, so you will need to hire a contractor somewhere down the line… but do you really? Perhaps during your own home ownership experience, you've had to oversee a few home improvement projects on your own.

These likely ranged from simple repainting jobs, to woodworking and everything in between. Whatever the case, it was cheaper to get it done by yourself and a few subcontractors instead of hiring a general contractor to do the job for you.

Unfortunately, the decision to push through as a DIY contractor might change if the house you're dealing with is going to be sold for a profit. But then again, getting it done DIY means you can cut back on the cost and increase your net profit. So what do you do?

There are a few things you can ask yourself if you want to find out whether you're ready to take on the job of a DIY contractor. Understanding where you stand in terms of these factors will give you a realistic idea regarding your readiness and capability to oversee the operations yourself.

☐ Do you have the time and availability to be present on site throughout the renovation process?

- ☐ Are you comfortable working with your hands and getting things done using power tools, construction materials, etc?
- ☐ Are the repairs and renovations required within your set of skills?
- ☐ Do you have contacts with subcontractors to do more tedious, technical jobs for you?
- ☐ Do you possess some knowledge on home improvement and renovation?
- ☐ Are you confident in your capability to generate outcomes comparable to a professional contractor given the tasks you intend to do yourself?

If you answered no to any one of these questions, then you might be better off seeking a pro. Look - we're not underestimating your capabilities and it's true that everyone can definitely learn to get home improvements done DIY-style. But taking a gamble with an investment could mean more expenses down the line.

If you end up botching up any part of the repairs, you might have to call in a pro anyway and end up making extra payments for more renovations than you initially required.

Even if you manage to get the repairs done all by yourself, there's the issue of quality. Does it look like something a potential buyer would be happy to see and pay for? Or will it likely deter prospective purchasers? If it doesn't really improve the saleability of your property, you'd have to get a contractor anyway to clean things up for you.

Don't let the allure of saving 10% - 30% on renovation costs get the best of you - you should know what's best for your property! If you feel that you're biting off more than you can chew, you probably are.

Start with Bare Minimum

Remember - you're not aiming to create the next Better Homes and Gardens featured property. So don't go overboard with the changes you want to make.

Generally, if you followed the right steps in the home selection process, the layout of your home should be suitable enough to work off of without having to change anything about the blueprint - which leads us to a guiding mantra in the process of fixing a flip.

Focus on the cosmetic.

Nicked paint, yellowish grout, broken tiles, leaky ceilings, old bathroom fixtures, creaky cabinet and cupboard doors, and other features that might make the home look unappealing should be the focus of your efforts. These don't make any changes to the overall footprint of the property and are generally cheaper to get done.

If you got your home from an auction and you weren't able to give it a closer inspection before sealing the deal, it's possible that you might find a few structural damages when you finally get to walk inside.

Issues concerning windows, weight-bearing beams, rotten walls, damaged roofing, and other features of the home that have something to do with the framework of the house can be a set back in terms of both time and cost. It's also worth mentioning that these repairs typically require different permits before they can be started. So that definitely adds to the expense on top of lengthening your timeline.

Again, it's worth reiterating that the house you choose will be pivotal to the profitability of your project. Make the wrong choice at the start and you might find yourself scrambling to figure out whether you can actually make a profit at all.

The 4 Kinds of Home Renovations

There are 4 different kinds of renovations that you can execute on your property, and each of these increase the value and saleability of your investment. Understanding which ones you need will help you come up with a plan that maximizes your property's AFV without having to spend too much of your budget.

The Basics

Basic renovations are changes and repairs that address features that buyers expect should be in good order. Ceilings that don't drip and leak in the rain, functional gutters and downspouts, a working furnace, and other basic aspects should be in good working condition if you want to attract buyers.

You don't necessarily have to renovate them all to the highest of standards - simple maintenance tasks and a few minor changes to get everything working can be more than enough.

Now the question - does basic renovation add value to your property? Not exactly. Buyers expect that houses for sale should have all of these basics in order to be considered viable options. Essentially, making sure that all of your investment's necessary features are operational simply brings your home up to standards.

So, should you get them done? Absolutely. If your home doesn't have all of these basics properly addressed, then you might not be able to reel in any buyers in the first place.

Curb Appeal

These renovations improve the aesthetic appeal of your property. Again, they don't necessarily add value but they will help make your house sell faster. Investing in these changes can make your property look handsome and inviting from the moment buyers take a glance, making it easier for them to visualize their life there and hopefully develop an attachment that drives profitable action.

Renovations that improve curb appeal include a well-manicured lawn, fresh coats of exterior and interior paint, clean carpets, and other cosmetic changes that make the place look neat and appealing.

Keep in mind though that there are some curb appeal changes that might only really appeal to you. So instead of trying to flex your interior design muscle, try to keep it simple. Neutral paint colors, a tasteful backsplash, and plain, clean bathroom tiles with white grout can be better than trying to impress buyers with your taste in unconventional bohemian inspired design.

Value-Adding

Now we move on to the aspect of renovation that actually improves the ARV of your investment. These changes focus on the features of the house that make it easier or more convenient to live in.

For instance, houses with updated HVAC systems that are eco-friendly and energy-efficient are likely to save its homeowner the added expense of clunky, outdated systems. The same goes for ranges and range hoods that are more efficient at saving electricity and eliminating foul odors from the interior space.

Value-adding renovations can be expensive at the get-go, so as a beginner, you might think they're not necessary. But because these changes can recoup up to 80% of their value once resale comes around, they can be incredibly beneficial for your endeavor.

Remember to stay within limits, though. Even if these changes add value, you don't want to be too different from the other houses in your vicinity. If you have state-of-the-art everything and the houses around just scream plain vanilla, your home might stick out... in a bad way.

Preferential

This house would look so much better with a game room in place of that third bedroom! Before you okay the renovation, ask yourself - is this something you prefer or is it a change that would get the thumbs up from anyone and everyone?

One major pitfall that many beginners succumb to when flipping their first house is treating it like home. The last thing you'd want is to make the mistake of developing an attachment to your investment, which might push you to make decisions that appeal more to your own sense of "practicality" and "improvement" instead of the market's concept of ideal.

Again, the best way to stay grounded when planning out those changes is by checking out the competition. If most of the houses for sale in the area have 3 bedrooms and no game rooms, you'd be better off following suit.

Other changes that fit into this category include hot tubs, wine cellars, swimming pools, and ponds. Not everyone wants them, and some of them might actually be a maintenance nightmare, making them a downside for practical buyers who want a home that's not hard to live in or to keep in good condition.

Putting Together Your Dream Team

One of the best ways to make sure you don't exceed your budget with each flip is to put together a professional team. These contractors and subcontractors will be the people you work with even on later projects, making it easier to stay on the same page regarding the changes you want to apply to your investment.

Putting together a solid team of home renovators can be tricky, especially if you're not necessarily familiar with the most prominent workers in your area. So you do have quite a bit of a lengthy process in front of you if you want to make sure you're getting the best.

Know What You Want

If you're not necessarily a home improvement pro, you might find it impossible to know exactly what needs to be changed or renovated when you first walk through your home. What you can do though is inspect any cosmetic changes that you feel are necessary and list these to come up with a general idea as to what you want to do with your house.

For more technical improvements, you might have to call in a professional who can give you a more accurate understanding of the specialized changes that need to happen. An architect, designer, or general contractor can be a good choice.

Scout for Your First Member

It's likely that the first professional you'll need on your team is an architect or designer. These pros can draw up constructional plans and help you get a better understanding of technical problems that need to be addressed. On top of that, these professionals can also look for contractors and subcontractors who can work on your project.

What you need to know however is that these services need to be paid for. So hiring an architect or designer to oversee your project can put a bit of a dent in your wallet, especially if you're going with someone who has more experience and credentials.

If you're not sure which professional you should on-board, it's okay. This simply means that there hasn't been anyone who has appealed to your specific standards and preferences just yet. So instead of rushing in to the hire, you might want to consider scouting your options. Once you do that, you can get a free consultation with each one to find out how much they'd charge and what they think needs to be done.

In doing this, you can compare their recommendations across the board. Are they all saying the same things? Are some architects pointing out changes that others feel aren't necessary? The ones who say that more repairs are necessary might actually be pointing out non-essential changes that they simply feel like recommending to bump up costs.

Ask Around

If you still haven't made a hire, don't worry. There's no harm in making sure you've got the right guys for the job. Another way to help improve your search and see all the available professionals who you might be able to work with is to ask around. People in the area are probably more aware of the more affordable yet reliable contractors and professionals that can help you with your project. You can ask friends in the area if they can recommend anyone, and maybe even ask if you can get preferred rates since you're being referred by someone that got services in the past.

If you worked with a real estate agent to find the house you purchased, they might also be able to provide some valuable input. After all, it would work in your favor if all the members of your team were familiar with each other to help keep a smooth flow of operations without the issue of personality clashes.

Narrow It Down

Now that you have a few favorites, it's time to narrow it down even further. The best way to do this would be to seek an interview with each professional you've found to find out what they can do for you, how much their services cost, and whether or not you feel that your personalities would click.

Sure, you're not looking for friends, so issues with personality traits should be the last of your concerns, right? Wrong. Working with people you can't see eye to eye with can make the entire renovation process taxing, tiring, and downright difficult. As a general rule, you should want to get along seamlessly with the people on your team especially because of the time-pressured situation of a house flip.

Compare the costs of each pro and assess whether you'd feel comfortable with the ones you've chosen. If you think you've found the right ones, then go ahead and make that hire.

Negotiate Fees

If your chosen contractors and professionals have fees that fit your budget perfectly, then there might not be a need to negotiate at all. Remember, it pays to be fair - these people are trying to make a living, so it would only be right to pay them the cost of their services. But if you find that some of the professionals on your roster charge a little more than the others, then you might be able to negotiate a more agreeable fee. This should help keep you within budget without having to start over the process of seeking out a suitable replacement.

Try to ask your team if they'd be willing to agree to a slightly lower price. To make it easier for them to agree, you can tell them that you plan to keep flipping houses as a long-term money-making strategy. That said, you will re-hire them for future projects, giving them a steady line of work even during supposed off seasons for their business.

Smart Tips for Renovating a Flip

When it comes to the renovation aspect of your project, the name of the game is cost reduction. The less you spend to get all of those changes out of the way, the more profit you'll make once you decide it's time to put your house up for sale.

Here are a few more money-saving strategies you can enact to help stay within or below budget without having to sacrifice the quality of your renovation.

Buy Power Tools

If you're planning to go big with DIY, then you might be better off buying power tools instead of renting them. Sure, it might seem more expensive now, but they'll be pretty much with you for as long as they're working. So you can offset their cost over a number of flips, not just the one you're working on right now.

Other than the contents of your standard toolbox, you should want to invest in a circular saw, reciprocating saw, nail gun, sander, drill, heat gun, and perhaps even a power washer to clean out decking and siding. Make sure you don't skimp out on their quality as well - the better the tools you buy, the longer they'll last in your care.

Ask for Remnant Materials

Visit your local construction supply shop and you might be able to get your hands-on discounted items by simply asking the clerks whether they have them stored in the back. Some buyers can be particularly detail-oriented when it comes to their purchases, so materials that have even the slightest dings, cracks, or imperfections often get sent back and replaced.

Stores keep these items in the back and hold them off until sale season, but you can get your hands-on them any time of the year by simply asking if they have any. These materials can be great for small projects, and a lot of these lightly used items can pass off as brand-new as long as you know how to mitigate their damages. (Also look out for scratch and dent appliances, they sell cheaper due to small dings and scratches.)

Weigh the Importance of Each Room

Did you know that the kitchen, master bathroom, and master bedroom are respectively the most important parts of a home for most buyers? These rooms have to have the best quality finishes, and drive prospects to their decision based on the appeal that each room offers.

That said, you can assume that the other rooms - bedrooms, living room, dining room, and other areas in the space - are of less importance and simply need to be clean and livable compared to the primary rooms of interest.

What this means for you is that you can cut back on costs by investing in premium materials for the kitchen, master bedroom, and bathroom. For other, less important rooms in the house, consider shelling out on builders-grade materials. These are much more affordable and can hold up fairly well if they're maintained properly, so they can work for most markets.

Hire Freelancers

Whatever the task, make sure to check out the freelance market since there can be some pretty impressive untapped talent there. These professionals work solo and often charge their own rate, making them much more affordable than hiring through agencies and construction companies.

Remember, large construction firms have equally large overhead costs. The cost of rent, utilities, admin workers, insurance, trucks, and other monthlies can mean that they have to weigh down their fees to meet all of their expenses while making a profit. So while they can provide you with all the services you need in one go, they can also sap your wallet of all its contents at the same time.

What you need to watch out for though when hiring freelancers is their insurance. Make sure they have coverage that pays out for accidental injury. Otherwise, you might have to deal with those costs as well in case they end up hurting themselves while working on your property.

Leverage Freebies

A lot of construction supply shops out there are trying to keep it competitive, so some of them will offer you a free design consultation if you end up purchasing a specific amount of product from them. So before you head out to the store, make sure you've got an all-inclusive list of all the things you need to purchase so you can meet that quota and get the free consult.

If you can have an in-store designer come to your property for free to help you with the plan, you might not need to hire an architect (win!) which helps reduce your expenses even more.

Choose One Shop and Stick to It

One thing that holds true for construction is that you won't always be able to purchase everything you need in one trip. Things will come up and changes will be made to the initial plan, requiring that you seek more material when the project is underway.

That said, you should make sure that you've settled on one specific construction supply shop where you intend to purchase all of the materials as you move through the renovation process. Scan the available retailers in your area and ask them for rewards and loyalty programs they might have to get a better understanding of where you can get the best value for your money.

Some construction supply shops might also team up with specific financial institutions like banks so that you can get special rebates if you use your credit card to make a purchase. If you're sure you can make those payments in full once your statement comes in the mail, then you can enjoy lots of impressive deals and promotions that aren't available through any other payment option or shop.

Ask About Overstocked Material

Storage is a powerful retail tool that most shops want to maximize. So you can be sure that construction supply stores will do anything to try to clear out storage space and make room for new, more profitable items.

When you search through the store for the items you need, approach a clerk and ask if they have any overstock materials of similar quality. They'd likely be happy to provide you a few options, since overstock and outdated items often eat up a lot of storage space, making it hard to take inventories and to stock up on items that are in demand.

As you might have guessed it, overstock items are often sold at a fraction of their original cost, so they do weigh a whole lot less on your budget without really getting stingy in terms of quality.

Establishing the Cost of Renovation

What's the point of all this saving if you have no idea as to the actual, measurable limits that you need to observe? Establishing the actual cost of renovation should happen before you get started on anything because it all factors in to the profit you'll make at the end of the endeavor. If you don't call the cost before beginning repairs, then you might find your profit to be much smaller once you make your sale.

The cost of renovations change from property to property because each house needs different repairs and changes. One way to get an estimate cost on renovations would be to take 10% of the price of the house when you purchased it. This should cover everything you need to pay for in order to flip the house. So if you purchased it for $300,000 USD, you should expect to allot a budget of $30,000 USD for repairs.

There are more accurate ways to come up with an estimate though. And this involves familiarizing yourself with the cost of materials at your local construction supply shop. Pay a visit to your chosen establishment and bring a pen and paper. List down all the materials you think you'd need to rehab a property and get both high and low costs based on the prices you see. Take this information home and organize it in a spreadsheet so you can easily access the details whenever you need them.

Next, go around and ask a bunch of contractors how much they charge for so and so. If you need a painting contractor, ask what he charges. The same goes for plumbers, exterminators, tiling, roofing, window, and other subcontractors you might need to help with your property. Get a bid from each one by outlining the kind of work you need done, and compare their prices across the board. Also make sure to state that you're looking for labor only prices, and that you will be the one supplying all the materials.

Now that you have all of this information, you might be able to come up with estimates for the different repairs you need. For instance, if a bucket of paint costs $24 USD and you need 2 buckets to paint each room in a 3 bedroom house, you'd need 6 buckets costing $144 USD. The painting contractor might charge you anywhere between $380 to $790 USD per room, which means you could pay between $1,140 USD to $2,370 USD to completely paint 3 bedrooms in your home. In total, the range for a painting job could be $1,284 to $2,514 - labor and materials included.

Now you've got both a high and low estimate, what you want to do is calculate the average cost, which in this case would be $1,899 USD. Perform the same estimations with the rest of the renovations you need and come up with a total cost.

Take this table for example:

REPAIR	LOW COST	HIGH COST
Paint bedrooms	$1,284	$2,514
Replace all carpets	$2,000	$2,500
Retile bathrooms	$700	$1,400
TOTAL COST	$3,984	$6,414
AVERAGE COST	$5,199	

Keep in mind that the estimate you get out of this method will still be highly speculative, and it may change depending on whether you choose more expensive materials and labor. You should also factor in the cost of permits and other fees when calculating your renovation cost. Sure, there's no way you can get the numbers for sure, but doing this can be much more realistic than simply assuming all the repairs would cost 10% of your investment's price at purchase.

How to Stay on Schedule

Aside from the actual expense associated with the hires, labor, and materials of the renovation itself, you also need to remember that time will have a large impact on your profit. The longer you hold on to a house, the longer you'll have to pay for its expenses. If you hold on it for too long, you might find that all the monthly payments you made completely offset your profit or leave you at a loss.

So making sure that the renovations run smoothly and according to schedule is an important facet of securing your profit and guaranteeing a fast flip.

Establish a Time Frame

Before calling up your friend for contractor recommendations, before going down to the local construction supply warehouse to list down prices, before even asking any professionals for their opinion - you need a time frame. Making sure that you allot enough time for each task will help keep you on track towards finishing your project as soon as possible.

1. Measure - The first thing that needs to be done is measuring the home. With an architect or design specialist, visit the house and map out the entire space. If the previous owner has a ready-made blueprint, this can eliminate the need to measure all together. Make sure it's intelligible and accurate though, and try to get it done in 2 weeks.

2. Conceptualize - Now, with your architect or designer, come up with the plan for renovation. This includes all necessary changes as well as drawing up a new floor plan to represent the house after the changes have been made. Be as specific as possible to eliminate confusion later on. Give yourself 2-3 weeks to finish the concept.

3. Budget and Finance - This step entails getting all the necessary estimates from suppliers and laborers, and consolidating all of that information into one solid number to help you establish the cost of your renovation. At this time, you might also seek out financing opportunities if you're not paying for the repairs from your own pocket. Give yourself 2-3 weeks for this.

4. Documentation - Once you've got your budget in order, it's time to secure all the permits and paperwork you need in order to properly and legally complete your renovations. If you need to go through zoning, you might end up spending more time on this step than you want to. So be thorough and ask all the questions before you proceed. Around 3-4 weeks should be enough to complete this task.

5. Construction - This final step involves sourcing your supplies, getting renovations built and performed, and making any necessary changes to the plan as you move along. Essentially, at the end of construction, you should have a house that's ready for sale. Of course, time frames can change depending on the scope of the repairs as well

as the efficiency of your team. But you can expect to be finished with construction between 6 weeks and 3 months.

Be Mindful of the Time

It's important to make sure that you're always aware of the phase of your renovation. Losing track of time, or planning certain aspects of the repairs without considering your time frame can cause you to lose precious weeks and make your flip much longer than you intended.

As a general rule, the first thing you need to consider is delivery dates. Larger construction materials like certain woods, tiles, and other necessities might not be readily available when you order them, so your supplier might have to put you on a delivery queue.

Ask for the estimated date of delivery so you can be present at the property when the trucks arrive. It also helps to know when the materials are coming so that you can instruct your team to be on site so they can get started with repairs as soon as the deliveries make their way through the door.

If you run into unexpected repairs (especially structural ones - yikes) as you go through renovations, ask your local municipal office whether there's any kind of red tape that might keep you from jumping on those structural damages ASAP. If they say that you need certain paperwork, try to get those done as soon as possible to prevent delays and address the repairs as soon as possible.

Hire a Project Manager

If you don't trust your own capabilities in overseeing a home renovation, you might want to look into hiring a project manager. These individuals are equipped with the skills necessary to keep a project - like a renovation - running on the dot. Of course, they might cost you more now, but they can help make sure that you won't have to wait too long for those repairs to finish.

At the start, it might be better for you to seek the assistance of a seasoned project manager. But as you continue to learn and grow in your expertise, you might be able to take the reins on your fix n' flips more confidently, especially when you learn the entire process of the renovation, as well as the necessary skills to efficiently see them through to completion.

Be Decisive

Eggshell blue or sandy fawn beige? Red-toned mosaic backsplash tiles or cobalt blue with intricate floral patterns? Decisions, decisions! Of course, we can't help but be critical when it comes to our choices - we want this house to look as good as possible! But remember, what you're aiming for is a timely completion, not a Pinterest-worthy design.

If you encounter any questions mid-way through your renovation, answer them quickly. Don't take your time sleeping on minor details that won't really affect the quality of the build. At the end of the day, what matters most is that you completed your renovation up to code and on schedule - all those smaller details about color and style can take a back seat.

True enough, the renovation part of the fix n' flip process can be the most tedious and toxic - but it's also often the most fun! During this phase, you can test your skills when it comes to handling people and projects, and improve your concepts of what makes a suitable, sellable home. As you continue to learn, you'll become more capable of making lightning-fast decisions for later flips, and you'll be able to confidently see through a renovation with little fuss.

Once that's all over though, things start to get technical. During the next part of the fix n' flip process, you'll encounter some more industry-specific ideas that might be difficult to grasp for first-timers. So grab that cup of coffee and limber up as we dive into the cut-throat scene of home selling.

CHAPTER 6:

IMPROVING THE FLIP

In order to successfully flip a property, you are going to need a team of experienced professionals. Before you begin analyzing deals, submitting offers and grabbing your hammer, take the time to set up your network first. This will help ensure your success.

Licensed Real Estate Agent

One of your first steps will be to locate a qualified real estate agent. Whether you decide to buy property from their Multiple Listing Service (MLS) or not, they will be a vital member of your network. A real estate agent will provide you with the following helpful services:

Submitting Offers to Purchase

Real estate agents are trained negotiators. Their purchase agreements are designed to legally protect you the purchaser. In addition, they will prepare, submit and track the offer for you freeing up your valuable time.

Plus, your buyer's agent is free! Agents receive payment through the seller's commission. So if you are making an offer on a MLS listing, why not use an agent that is working in your behalf rather than putting the offer through the agent that is working for the buyer (and not you).

Presenting CMAs

Do you have the time, the training and the resources to record, track and measure all the properties that have sold in your market area over the past 12 months? Probably not. But your agent has them all stored in a nice neat database and they would be more than happy to prepare a Comparative Market Analysis (CMA) for you.

The purpose of a CMA is to determine the most likely sales price of a property by comparing (and adjusting) recent similar sales in the neighborhood. When you combine the agent's experience and knowledge of the market along with this data, you have an invaluable resource to make sure that you are not paying too much for a property.

Determining Your ARV

What is an ARV you ask? It stands for the "After Renovation Value" or "After Repair Value." In effect, it is the most likely sales price of your property after you have repaired, remodeled or renovated it. This is the critical number upon which all your estimates, calculations and profits will be based on. You do not want to take a guess. You definitely do not want to be wrong.

Having a professional who can prepare that number with accuracy is absolutely worth it.

Locate Buyers

Real estate agents who have been in the business for many years will have a large network of buyers and contacts.

How to choose a good real estate salesperson?

Not all salespeople are the same. Some are little better than a used car salesman and others have been in the business so long that they are a trusted professional that even appraisers admire (and that is saying a lot). Here are a few tips to help with the interview process:

- Use only agents that work in the business full-time.
- Look for someone who has been in the business for at least 5 years.
- How many transactions (buying or selling) did they complete last year?
- Would they be willing to complete CMAs and ARVs on properties you are interested in purchasing?
- Check with a few past clients. If they were satisfied then probably you will be too.

If the agent will charge you for completing a CMA or ARV, do not act shocked or offended. They have no doubt met many fly-by-night "investors" that only wasted their time. Assure them that you would only ask for their advice and opinions on properties that you are seriously considering – and then be willing to pay their fee (which is generally around $100).

Licensed Contractors

Unless you have a contractor's license and plenty of skills and experience in rehabbing houses, you are going to need a contractor. Not only will they be used for some, if not all, of the project, but their initial inspection of the property and their comments about it will be critical to your evaluation.

You will likely need several different contractors to do different parts of the job. For right now, concentrate on getting a general contractor in your network. They will no doubt be able to recommend others as you need them. Your real estate agent will also know of others who have good and honest reputations.

How to Find a Good Contractor

When you are renovating a house, the job needs to be done right – the first time. A buyer is going to demand quality construction. The quality of the work will have a direct correlation to the sales price of the property.

That being said, stay away from the handyman type contractors. These are the guys that generally do work on the side. Often they are not licensed or insured. Though they may be cheaper, it will show in their work and if something goes wrong, you will have little recourse.

Instead, look for licensed, bonded and insured builders or general contractors that have years of experience in their field. Ask for a list of testimonials and phone numbers of some recent clients and check to see if they were satisfied with the work. Also check with their clients on the ability to keep a reasonable timetable.

How to Get the Best Quality of Work from Your Contractor

One of the easiest way to ensure that your contractor completes everything that you have in mind is to get all bids in writing and then pay attention to the detail. If the contractor says he will paint the exterior, find out if the price includes pressure washing. Will it cover painting the doors and trim and all outbuildings? Getting these details in writing will save you and the contractor a ton of stress.

Home Inspector

Buyers nearly always opt to hire a home inspector to look over the property before they waive their purchase contingencies. Though you cannot recommend that they use your inspector, having one as part of your network will come in handy – for two reasons.

The Purchase Property Inspection

Though you will have a contractor as part of your team, a property inspector can come in handy as well. If you are looking at a quick flip or a home that appears to only need superficial improvement, a general contractor may not be necessary – but a complete inspection is. This is a good time to bring in the home inspector. They are going to carefully examine the property and look for things that you could easily miss.

The Pre-Sales Inspection

Imagine the expression on the buyer's face when they receive their inspector's report on your property with a list of 25 items. You know they are a list of nit-picky things that have no real effect on safety or value, but now the seller is insisting that your property is not worth your asking price and the deal falls through.

I would have saved you a world of trouble by getting an inspection completed before you list the home for sale. In this way, you can take care of everything that the inspector finds. When your buyer receives the report from his inspector, he will be surprised to see a home in pristine condition.

How to Choose a Home Inspector

You want an inspector that is both thorough and trustworthy. Here are a few questions you will want to know the answer to before he joins your team:

Are you licensed or a member of a home inspector association?

In many states, you do not have to be licensed to be a home inspector. Inspectors who are members of either ASHI (American Society of Home Inspectors) or NAHI (National Association of Home Inspectors) must adhere to a code of ethics and demonstrate expertise and competency.

Do you have a contractor's license?

Locate a home inspector that either is or was a general contractor. They will have a much better grasp of construction techniques, problems and building codes.

How long have you been a home inspector?

It takes many years of experience and training to develop the skills and insight needed to be a good home inspector.

Do you carry Errors and Omissions (E&O) Insurance?

If the inspector misses a major problem, their E&O insurance can help you to recover your damages. Never hire an inspector that does not have this type of insurance.

CHAPTER 7:

TYPES OF FINANCING

Getting Financing

If life were a dream, we would all have enough cash under our mattress to buy a house and pay for its renovation. But unfortunately, that is only a fantasy for those starting out in the business. So, we are going to analyze a couple of ways you could get funding to purchase and renovate your fix-and-flip.

Obtaining conventional financing as a multi-property buy-and-hold investor can be a challenge on its own, but getting conventional short-term financing is near to impossible. Property flippers typically are looking at financing that will extend no more than 12 months with a target of less than six.

National lenders make their money on their ability to sell loans to the secondary mortgage market. Fannie Mae and Freddie Mac are only interested in long-term loans. Thus, to obtain conventional financing, you will need to find a lender that will hold the loans in house.

Conventional Financing

Obtaining conventional financing is perhaps the "safest" way to pay for a property flip – besides paying cash. In-house loans are going to be backed, not by the Federal government, but by the equity in the home and your personal credit worthiness. A good place to start shopping around is to visit local banks and credit unions. They often write short-term portfolio loans.

In order to qualify for these types of loans, you are going to need to meet stricter lending requirements and will most likely need a larger down payment. You must have a good credit score for starters. You should shoot for a score of 620 or above. You will get a lower interest rate if you are in the 700s.

When looking for a lender, go meet with several. Be upfront with them about what you plan to do and how you will go about it and how long you expect the loan will be active. Be prepared to share your real estate experience and/or a list of qualified team members. Work to become pre-qualified. This will help you narrow down your property choices and speed up the closing process.

If you decide to go conventional, make sure that your loan does not have a prepayment penalty. Many conventional loans also carry a restriction on when you can resell the property. There can be some really hefty penalties for a violation, so watch out!

Hard Money Loans

Hard money loans (HML) are short-term, non-bank loans that are made by a company or private investor. The loan is guaranteed more by the property and less on the credit of the borrower. Hard money loans are used by savvy investors all the time. It is a tried and true way to finance a fix-and-flip.

When you know exactly what you are getting into and factor in the higher-than-average loan costs into your formula, it can be a great resource. If, however, you do not honestly weigh the risks, it can be a deal breaker. Why?

Hard money loans can be extremely expensive and need to be carefully factored into your profitability calculations. These lenders charge extremely high interest rates (14 -20%), carry multiple points (up to 10) and have high closing costs. Points are paid upfront with each point equaling 1% of the loan amount. But, they are perfect for short term loans.

The loans are usually made off the After Repair Value (ARV) and have a loan-to-value ratio of between 55% and 75% based on the borrower's credit score. This can pick up any purchase equity (unlike conventional mortgages) and include funding for repairs. Notice how it works in the following comparison:

Purchase Price	$100,000
Market Value	$120,000

ARV	$175,000	
	Conventional Loan	Hard Money Loan
Loan	80% of Purchase Price	70% of ARV
Loan Amount	$80,000	$122,500
Down Payment	20% of Purchase Or 10-20% of Purchase or	
	$20,000	$122,500

Use a HELOC

Do you have equity sitting in your personal residence or in another investment property? If so, then consider accessing this equity through a Home Equity Line of Credit (HELOC). A HELOC is superior to an Equity Loan because the loan amount is more like a credit card limit than a bank loan. You can borrow up to the maximum loan amount, pay it back and then borrow again without having to go through the lending process each time.

These loans will only allow a maximum total loan-to-value of 80% which will include your first mortgage and the HELOC.

For example, if your home is worth $250,000 and you have a mortgage on it for $145,000. The maximum you could pull out using a HELOC would be $55,000 ($250,000 x .80 = $200,000 - $145,000 = $55,000). This can be a great way to finance repairs on a property.

The interest rate is higher than a conventional mortgage but the closing costs are less. But... if you are borrowing against your personal residence and the deal goes sour, make sure you have the monthly income to cover the additional loan payment.

Owner Financing

Buying a property on a land contract (also known as owner financing) can be a great way to finance a short-term purchase. Many property owners wouldn't mind making a little extra on the sale of their home. It can be a real win-win situation.

Instead of getting a mortgage, you would make monthly payments to the owner. A down payment is made at the time of closing which is generally less than 10%. The owner will charge interest which is usually one or two percentage points above conventional mortgage rates (perhaps higher because of the short term nature of the loan). When you are ready to resell the property, the remainder of the loan balance is paid to the original owner and you keep the profit.

This is a good option if you are lacking financing for a down payment. The owner could carry a mortgage on the property in the second position with the conventional financing being in the first. You would need to figure out, though, how to pay for the repairs.

Another option to use owner financing is to purchase the property "Subject To" the existing mortgage. The buyer pays the seller the difference between the purchase price and the mortgage balance. He then takes over the payments to the seller's mortgage. Though most mortgages contain a "due on sales clause," many lenders simply overlook this as long as the payment is made on time.

Most homeowners, however, do not like this option because they take a risk that the buyer – you – will not make the payments on time and hence trash their credit. Sellers who are quick to take this offer are usually ones that are already behind in their mortgage payments and are facing foreclosure.

Borrow from an IRA

We have talked about accessing your own home's equity or getting a hard money loan from a private investor, but did you know that you can finance real estate with either a self-directed IRA or a 401(k)? You can use your personal account or that of a private investor.

In order to use a retirement account to fund real estate, the IRA must be a custodial account. The repayment terms and payment schedule needs to be in writing and all payments, including the interest, would go back into the IRA. The beautiful part is that since IRAs are tax-exempt, the loan is either tax-free or tax-deferred based on the IRA type.

You should consult with an experienced advisor before trying to set this up since there are some very specific rules and regulations governing property purchases.

Getting Prepared

Since your loan is going to be based not only on your credit worthiness but also on the ROI on the investment, you are going to want to show a lender – regardless of who they are – that you know what you are doing and are aware of the costs and risks.

Once you have decided on your type of financing and hopefully gotten pre-qualified or at least pre-approved, you will no doubt need more evidence to finalize the loan. This will include a copy of the purchase agreement, contract with your contractor, multiple estimates of renovation costs, a marketing plan, anticipated holding costs and the projected time to completion.

You will need to be prepared to answer some hard questions such as:

How much experience do you have on such projects?
How much of your personal funds are you using for this project?
What happens if the construction costs are more than you estimated?
What is your fall back or exit plan if the house does not sell in time?

Would you be able to qualify for a conventional mortgage if the property does not sell?

CHAPTER 8:

WORKING WITH REALTORS

There are many advantages to working with a realtor, but there are also a few disadvantages. While the role of a realtor is one you can do yourself, having a realtor do it for you provides you with a multitude of resources that you otherwise wouldn't have. When first starting out, working with a realtor will save you from the inevitable mistakes of the learning curve.

Understanding the Selling Process

Working with a realtor will make selling your house much easier for you. They will walk you through the process, do a majority of the work, and provide you with access to their professional resources and networks. That being said, understanding the selling process and everything they do will help you to better appreciate their role and effort in the flipping process. Many people see paying a realtor as an unneeded expense, and for those that have the know-how and resources, it may indeed be an unneeded expense. However, for the majority of new house flippers, it is a very necessary expense.

Setting a Price

The first thing your realtor will be doing is determining a selling price range for the house. This process involves touring the house and taking notes regarding the features of the house including size, number of bedrooms, number of bathrooms, and extra selling features such as a porch, central air, outdoor storage, etc. The realtor will take all this information and then look at comparables in the area.

The realtor is trained to identify which properties in the area are really comparable to the house you are selling. Being a comparable property means more than being the same approximate size or having the same number of bedrooms. Comparables cover a wide range of features. In some cases, it is difficult to find true comparables. In these situations, your realtor will rely on what information is available to her, along with what she knows about the market and what features influence the selling price. For example, regardless of neighborhood, brick houses sell for more than non-brick houses and corner lots sell for more than non-corner lots. These are the kinds of features your realtor will take into account when suggesting a price for your house.

Stage the House

Once a price is set, the target market for the house will have already been identified. The realtor will then work with you to stage the house in a way that will appeal to the target market. Many realtors may already have the furniture and accessories to stage the house themselves, or they may have a professional stager on their team of people. Either way, the realtor will ensure the house is staged in a way that will appeal to prospective buyers, highlight the house's more desirable features, and give the impression of spacious, low-maintenance living.

Make sure the pictures are not taken until after the house has been staged. This will make your marketing material stronger and more enticing.

Once the house is clean and staged, the realtor will walk through the house and around the property taking pictures of everything. These pictures will be used in the marketing material for the house. The realtor may also choose to create a video tour of the house to post online, if doing so is one of her normal marketing tactics. Either way, your realtor will work to create images of the house that will be both appealing and enticing. The goal of posting images and videos online is to get people to want to visit the property.

Market the House

Your realtor will then start marketing your house. She will get the house on the Multiple Listing Service (MLS), which allows all other realtors in the area to see the house. This is beneficial because it allows other realtors to also market your house if they have clients looking in the area and your house fits their criteria. Your realtor will also use the pictures she took to create fliers and fact sheets. She will write descriptions of the house for prospective buyers. She will also promote the house through her company's online and offline channels.

Arrange an Open House and Showings

Your realtor will schedule an open house, which is an opportunity for prospective buyers to come look at the house and ask any questions they may have about the house. Open houses are generally two-hour events. The realtor will also arrange showings with interested prospective buyers and other realtors that have prospective buyers. Your realtor will stay available with little notice to show the house when the opportunity arises. Since you don't live in the house, this will be zero-stress or frustration for you.

Targeting Your Market

When trying to sell a house, there are two markets you need to consider: the housing market and your target market. Your target market are the buyers that are most likely to want to buy your house based on size, location, and price. Your realtor will have a solid understanding of both, and additionally what you need to do in order to sell your house quickly. There are strategies for both dealing with the housing market and the target market in a productive way.

Target the Housing Market

The housing market will not only dictate how you are able to price your house, but also how you need to approach negotiations. Once the price is set, and you start getting offers, your realtor can help you go through each offer to decide which is the best option for you. Your realtor will also be able to help you decide when you should counter and when you should accept the offer on the table. Based on his understanding of the market, your realtor will have a pretty good idea of how much you can realistically get for the house.

Target Your Potential Buyers

Targeting potential buyers is also important when setting the price and staging the home. For example, if you are selling a house with three or more bedrooms in a good school district with a good size yard, you can assume you will have people with families looking at the house. With that in mind, you can stage at least one of the bedrooms to be a kids' bedroom, as opposed to a home office or guest room. Additionally, while showing the house, your realtor can point out the school system, the house's proximity to parks, and other kid attractions.

If you are a licensed realtor you can always put your flip on the Multiple Listing Service (MLS). Of course, you will pay a commission to the buyers' broker if you decide to do that, so you might want to try some marketing yourself first. Here are some suggestions that have worked well for other flippers.

Neighborhood Blog

Most neighborhoods have a blog where people can advertise anything they have for sale, their businesses and services, and even a lost pet. The blog is also a good way to market your flip. Use the neighborhood blog and start far ahead of time so that you can encourage people to pay attention to the status of the improvements. Create curiosity and invite people to pay you a visit and see the home. As soon as you've completed all the renovations, have a presale open house for all the neighbors to come. Or, hold a block party to celebrate the completion. Cook out some burgers and hotdogs, and get the neighbors together for a party and invite them to tour the home.

When you post on the neighborhood blog, be sure also to add pictures of your progress. It can be fun to do before and after photos as well. Every time you get some things delivered, take a picture of the workers installing the beautiful things you have purchased for your flip. When you are ready to hold the home open for the neighbors, show pictures of the staged home, and let them know they can purchase the furnishings as well. Most of all, make it a fun afternoon.

Contact residents in the surrounding neighborhoods and let them know you have a home to sell nearby. Ask if they have a community blog, and if so would they mind letting their neighbors know about your open house? Most people are happy to help and are curious about your home.

Put A "For Sale By Owner" Sign Out Front

If you put it in the MLS right away, put your brokerage sign out front and attract as many buyers as you can from the sign so that you can refer to another agent in your office and collect referral fees. You can also do this with a "For Sale By Owner" sign. You'll be receiving a lot of calls from interested buyers, and you can refer those as well. A simple way to get their number is to put them off for a moment. You might say something like this. "I'm sorry, but I'm on the phone with another person interested in the home. Let me take down your name and number, and I'll give you a call as soon as I hang up, okay?" They want to know about the home, so they'll be happy to leave their contact information.

When you give them a callback, don't try to sell the home over the phone. It will only give the prospects an opportunity to find some reason they don't want to buy. Instead, let them know you're planning on being at the house that day. Tell them even though you'll be selling the furniture when you sell the home, you are still excited to see how it looks with all the new furniture inside, and then invite them to meet you at the house. If nothing else, they'll come to see the furniture and then perhaps fall in love with the house. Or, they might know someone else who would be interested.

If they come with a realtor, all the better. You can market to their realtor as well. If they are not represented by an agent but aren't interested in purchasing your flip, that's okay too. If you have another flip in the area, show them. If not, take down their contact information and refer them to a realtor in your office.

If you are not licensed but often work with a preferred realtor, refer them to that person so that you can continue to develop healthy relationships. Or, if you know of any other investment properties in the area, let the buyers know you have a home in mind that sounds like it might be perfect for them. Get their contact information, and then refer the customer to another investor. They'll return the favor, and you'll both develop a relationship that will teach you a lot and be mutually beneficial. Some investors who flip several houses at once try to get them close together so they can show all of them to buyers who visit just one.

Fliers & Local Newspapers

A lot of smaller cities have a local newspaper where it is affordable to market your property. Or, you can place an insert in the paper and advertise all your flips at the same time. Be sure to include colorful pictures of the inside and outside to entice buyers, and promote when you are holding the homes open. If you don't have any other homes in the area, you might want to do some cooperative advertising with another investor close by and share in the marketing costs. If you decide to include some of the furnishings, let the buyers know that they won't be available until after the close of the home.

If you are putting signage out front, include your fliers or ads in a holder attached to the sign. Add more pictures than information. Don't answer all the buyer's questions on the posted flyer. You need to give them a reason to call. Be sure to make the phone number bigger and bolder on the flyer, so it's easy to find. If you are licensed, be sure to have the approval of your broker for all the information that needs appear in the fliers.

Neighborhood Yard Sale

If you want all the neighbors to see the home first, you ought to hold a neighborhood yard sale. Get as many neighbors involved as possible, put up a ton of signs advertising multiple family yard sale, and then put out your open house signs with advertisements for the furnishings as well. Make it a celebration with balloons, a cookout, and a lot of excitement and enthusiasm. Serve the neighbors lunch as they work their yard sales.

Yard sales are a good time for potential buyers to tour the house and see how friendly and welcoming the neighbors are. Plus, it's a party atmosphere, and everybody loves a party.

Craigslist

As you advertise the yard sales, put it on Craigslist as well. You might want to post some pictures of the inside and outside of the house and then say there is a ten-family block yard sale, including free hotdogs and hamburgers, and everything must go, including the house. Prepare to have a lot of traffic through the house. It might be a good idea to put down some plastic in the high-traffic areas to protect the carpet. Or, set out that box of booties and encourage everyone to cover their shoes.

Passing out some fliers to local realtors® ahead of time is also an excellent idea. Let them know they'll have first chance at the home before it goes into MLS. You might even want to contact the broker/owner to arrange an office tour of the home. Give some fliers to your title company as well. Title companies often tour homes for the investors and realtors® who frequently use their services, so sign up for one of their tours.

You should also be developing relationships with other investors who are flipping houses. If so, be sure to email fliers to them and let them know about your open house. You might even ask them to send buyers that are not interested in their home your way.

Local Retailers

If you have a few smaller strip centers near your flip, it's always fun to take a little glass container of chocolates with a picture of your flip wrapped around the jar. Ask if you can leave some flyers of the home as well, and be sure to ask for a few cards of theirs to pass out to all those who tour your home. Let them know they'll be able to hand-pick their customers.

Multiple Listing Service (MLS)

If you don't get much action with your marketing efforts, then list it and get the home in the MLS. Give yourself two to three weeks of marketing before you do so. The first few weeks a home is on the market are the best to attract willing and able buyers. If you have begun your marketing efforts in advance of your planned opening, you should generate a lot of interest.

While your home is in the process of selling, you should be out there looking for a new home to flip to continue to grow your house flipping business.

CHAPTER 9:

REHABBING AND GETTING READY FOR THE SALE

Now you have your house and the most exciting part is here. This is where your budget and your timeline come into play. All the work is beginning and you are going to transform your house into profit! Let's go over some tips and tricks to get you through the next few weeks.

Curb Appeal

The very first thing you should do is create curb appeal to draw attention to your house right away. The best part is you can do this yourself which will save you some cash. Mow the lawn, paint the front of the house if necessary, maybe spruce it up and add a splash of color. Plant some flowers or bushes and clean up the yard. A little further down the road you will want to put out your for-sale sign but not until you are at least 60%-70% done with the rehab. Even though your house won't be ready for a few weeks it is beneficial to generate as much interest as possible as early as possible. If you can get a buyer before the reno is complete you are way ahead of the game and will save a ton of money on maintaining the house until you can find a buyer.

The Renovations

There are three main components to your renovation; scope, schedule and cost. Scope is the work that needs to be done, schedule is the estimated time it will take to complete each project individually and the renovation and cost which is how much materials and labor will cost plus a contingency.

It is a good idea to have a meeting with your contractor, subcontractors and any other vital team members before the project begins. This is the time for you to develop your SOW (Scope of Work) which is a detailed itinerary of your plan. This is a perfect time to hash out all the logistics before you move forward so there is no confusion as the project continues. You should continually have these meetings so you and your team can stay on the same page and keep the lines of communication open. You want to be as involved as you can, even if you don't know a lot about construction. This is part of the learning process and the more time you spend involved in your project, the more you will know on each next flip.

You also want to have a contingency plan. You have your direct costs (materials and labor) and your carrying costs, however there is always something else. There could be unforeseen problems like asbestos, mold or a structural problem that is going to throw a wrench in your perfectly laid plans. Take the estimate from your contractor and add 10%. That is your contingency plan. If you don't spend it all then it just goes right back into your pocket.

When you first do a walk through with a home inspector he will give you a detailed list of what needs to be fixed. You and your contractor can use this list as the starting point for your rehab. Getting your house up to code should be the first priority for your contractor.

There are four major things to look for. These four are the most expensive and require permits. The roof, plumbing, structure and electrical should be the four main things you examine before signing on the dotted line. A radon test is also important as both a buying tool and selling tool. Radon is a radioactive gas that is found in one of every fifteen houses in America. Radon is extremely tricky and expensive to get rid of. Issues with any of these can end up costing you a fortune in repairs, permits and labor. Avoiding extremely old houses is a good rule to follow unless you are rolling in dough and want a long, expensive flip. This is why you should walk through the house with your contractor before purchasing it and make sure he is writing and not just talking.

Once you and your team have a starting point and know what basic repairs need to be made you can start going over the improvements necessary to update the house and make it appealing for sale.

You should be renovating not just according to your budget but according to your target market as well. You don't need to go overboard with recessed lighting and marble countertops if your house is in a blue-collar neighborhood. So, what is your target market looking for in a house? Well since your first flip is probably in a middle to lower middle class probably just a clean, functional and, most of all, affordable house. Check out some of the houses in the neighborhood. Are they carpeted or hardwood floors? Are the kitchens open concept? Is crown molding a popular choice? Rehab your house so it will be comparable to the others. If a lot of millennials are flocking to that area, find out what they are buying. If you don't cater to your market you will end up sitting on the house a long time.

Once you are finished (or think you are finished) with the renovations, the home inspector will come again to make sure everything is up to code. You can then make any last-minute fixes that need to be completed before the appraisal. The appraisal usually happens a week or two after the completion of the renovations. He and your real estate agent will work together to get an accurate ARV. Then you can nail down your asking price and sell it.

Tips to help offset the cost of rehab

You should plan on having multiple jobs going on at once. You don't need to wait until one thing is done to start the other.

Hiring multiple contractors or handymen can get the work done a lot faster.

Finding cheap or alternative materials can save you thousands of dollars. Check out recycled materials stores like ReStore. You can also frequently find discounted materials at Home Depot and Lowe's- just ask a floor associate to show you what they have. You wouldn't believe the amount of cheap and perfectly good materials you can find on Craigslist. Not only does this save you a ton but it is good for the environment! Ask your contractor if he has any leftover materials from another job that you can buy from him at a discounted rate.

Use imitation materials when you can. Buy cheaper wood and just paint or stain it. Use a good laminate instead of real hardwood. You can buy affordable fixtures that will give an upgraded look to cabinets, bathrooms and more. Don't gut and rehab a bathroom when you can transform it with a new vanity from Home Depot for $100 and save yourself hundreds of dollars.

Find out what you can do yourself. Not only will you save yourself some money but it is great hands-on learning. Even if you are not a handyman you can probably still paint a wall, install cabinet fixtures or hang new blinds yourself. However, do not try anything that is beyond your skill level. Leave it to the professionals to ensure a quality job.

Avoid the plumbing. This isn't to say don't get it up to code and working, but don't make any grand plans to move faucets, toilets, etc. This is extremely costly and time consuming. Work with what you have. Again, this is not your house.

It may sound silly but watching the latest home improvement and DIY shows will give you lots of ideas and trends that are current. A lot of these shows have affordable ways to achieve up to date style and often are simple things that you might be able to do yourself like adding some backsplash tiles to the kitchen or painting an accent wall in the bedrooms. The demolition is easy and can be done by you plus it is a lot of fun!

And remember, it's not your house so don't fall in love with it! While your first flip is going to be the most exhilarating, getting carried away can be really easy to do. Your instinct will be to rehab and remodel according to your dream house. Keep in mind that this is not for you! You may want to gut and build the most beautiful kitchen in the world, but it will be a total waste of money since you are going to sell it. Stay grounded and distance yourself emotionally and personally from your flip house. When you make a boat load of money from flipping you can have your jacuzzi bathtub installed in your own home.

There is a cheaper alternative to renovating though it is not a popular one. Some flippers choose to buy a house that is in okay condition and clean it up aesthetically then sell it without doing any real renovations. This kind of flip entails painting and fixing the glaring details of a house so it is presentable. You then sell the house with the bare minimum of renovations for a profit. While ethically this is not the best choice, it does turn a profit quickly and efficiently.

CHAPTER 10:

MARKETING YOUR HOUSE TO SELL

Marketing your house to sell is an invaluable process. You already know the faster you are able to sell the property, the faster you will recoup your investment and make a profit. The housing market can be a competitive one, which is why it is essential to effectively market your house across multiple channels simultaneously. Marketing includes both online and offline activities. You don't need to be a marketing professional to effectively market your house, but you do need to understand what works and what doesn't.

Strategies That Work

When considering your different options in marketing, you want to focus on the strategies that are effective while also being cost efficient. When deciding how to market the house, talk to your realtor first, if you are working with one. Your realtor should certainly be able to help tremendously with this part, as it is also in his best interest to sell the house quickly. There are three options in offline marketing that you should consider: print advertising, yard signs, and networking.

Print Advertising

This includes advertising in local papers and house sale magazines. This type of advertising can be costly depending on the area you are living in. However, if you are planning a large open house, you may want to take the chance. A lot of people still check the newspaper when looking for local open houses. Print advertising is also a great way to get your name out there. This is helpful if you really build your flipping business and have houses to sell on a regular basis.

Check the difference in price between a printed classified ad and an ad with a picture included. Publishing ads with pictures is more effective because it catches the reader's attention and stands out among all the other ads. However, it can also be very expensive.

Yard Signs

Yard signs have proven to be very effective. For many people thinking about buying a house, it is not uncommon to drive around the neighborhoods where they want to live in search of "For Sale" signs. Sometimes people aren't necessarily looking to buy a house, but simply driving through a neighborhood they really like and see a "For Sale" sign. Yard signs also encourage word-of-mouth marketing. Neighbors are more likely to tell people they know are looking to buy a house. Yard signs can be purchased for a relatively inexpensive price at a hardware store or through a printing company. You can even order generic "For Sale" signs featuring your company name and contact information, so the same sign can be used over and over again. If you are working with a realtor, they likely already have signs that can be used at your property, so this will be a non-expense.

Networking

Another important form of marketing that people often overlook is networking. Let people know you have a house for sale. Offer a referral fee to anyone who finds you a legitimate buyer. See if there are any professional organizations in your area that cater to landlords or other property investors. For example, in Lorain County, Ohio, there is an organization called the Lake Erie Landlord Association. They have monthly meetings and part of their monthly meeting is what they call "Buy, Sell, and Trade." This is a time when members can stand up and make announcements regarding properties they have for sale. Other members may be interested in buying the house or they can help spread the word. These types of organizations can be crucial to your long-term success as a house flipper.

Accurately Pricing the House

While this may not be an obvious marketing strategy, it is probably one of the most important. Accurate pricing is essential in order to get people to actually visit the house for a showing. Houses that are priced too high will sit on the market because there are too many other options selling for better prices. Houses that are priced too low might sell quickly, but you'll be losing money on the opportunity. Plus, you might have people who don't look because they assume with such a low asking price, there must be something wrong with the house.

Strategies to Avoid

Just as there are successful strategies that you should focus on when marketing your house, there are strategies that you should avoid. These strategies aren't necessarily ineffective, but their level of effectiveness is not enough to justify the time, energy, and money that goes into them.

Television Realty Shows

Some realty companies still air television shows where they showcase the houses they have for sale. While seeing your house on television might be fun, it is hardly an effective strategy. The market for those shows is very narrow and depending on how you get showcased, it can be expensive. When compared to online advertising outlets, the television shows are archaic.

Flier Boxes

You can get a clear plastic box to put outside the house for fliers. These are ineffective for several reasons. First, the fliers tend to be taken by anyone walking down the street. People grab them out of curiosity and then don't put them back. Also, fliers get ruined after the first rain because the boxes are not water sealed. As long as your yard sign has the needed contact information on it, there is no reason an interested buyer would need a flier on the spot. If someone walking by is really interested, they can look the house up online or call the number provided to get more information.

There is some debate over the effectiveness of flier boxes. If you are working with a realtor that swears by them and they are covering the cost of the fliers, it's worth trying. Even if it doesn't help, it won't cost you anything.

Creating Your Own Website

Even though you're starting out with just one property, you want to be prepared for your business to grow quickly. Starting a website now will enable you to start building your online presence, so that when you have houses for sale, you are already established online. Additionally, you can advertise other companies through your website and make your website independently profitable as part of your overall business.

Setting Up a Website

The first step to creating your own website is choosing a domain name that will accurately represent your company and is available through domain registries. Once you find a domain name, you will need to buy it to ensure no one else will.

The second step is to set your website up with a content management system (CMS). Popular CMSs include WordPress and Joomla. These offer drag and drop features, which allow you to design your own website without really knowing HTML. While there may still be situations where you will need specialized design with HTML, you can hire someone to handle that for you.

Once your website is published, you'll need to start adding content. This is also something you can hire out relatively inexpensively. Until you start having houses ready to sell, you can build your website by adding content to a blog on your website. Your blog can cover topics related to real estate, selling houses, staging houses, and flipping houses. This will help you grow a reader base.

Advertising Houses Through Your Website

When you do have a house ready to sell, you can post all your house's information on your website. As you post ads on other websites, you can include links back to your website. You can also set up an interactive calendar, which would allow people to schedule a showing right from your website, or if you are working with a realtor, you can have a link to your realtor's contact information.

It is important to keep your website regularly updated. New content should be added at least a couple times a week. Search engines monitor web activity when choosing relevant websites for search results.

Is Internet marketing really that important?

These days, Internet marketing is essential. You can't just stick a sign out front and hope for the best. You need to be highly proactive, and Internet marketing is the most effective way to do that.

Internet Marketing

Internet marketing has become a significant source of marketing for real estate. Many buyers, particularly young buyers, are looking online before contacting realtors or sellers. They want to gather as much information as they can to make an informed decision more quickly. For that reason, it is essential that you have an online marketing strategy, and you make sure all the vital information regarding the properties you have for sale is easily accessible online.

Content Marketing

Content marketing refers to the marketing of content you create and post online. This can include written content, images, and videos. Content marketing, if done correctly, can be highly effective. The one downside to marketing a house online yourself is that the big realty companies already have a significant amount of clout online in regard to search engine rankings, so you will need to work harder to be seen.

The first thing you want to do is write a detailed description of the property. Write a description of each room and significant feature in the house. You want to use a lot of descriptive words to make the house sound as amazingly inviting and desirable as possible. You then need to take your written description, the images you took and edited for marketing purposes, and the video you created, and post them online in as many different places as you can.

Writing Sales Copy

Writing sales copy is an industry of its own. It is a way of writing that makes the product appeal to consumers on a psychological level. Copywriters are well trained in how to use descriptive words and phrases to get an emotional reaction out of readers. While you can't learn how to be an effective copywriter overnight, you can pursue ways to improve the quality of your descriptions. To do this, you can hire a copywriter to write your descriptions for you. You can learn basic copywriting and do it yourself, or you can hire a copywriter, who is willing to work with you to help you improve your own descriptions. The path you choose will depend on how much time and money you want to invest in getting this done. This is one example of when it might be best to preserve your time for more important tasks and hiring someone to write the descriptions for you.

Social Media Marketing

Social media marketing is another effective branch of online marketing. To market your house through social media, you need to strategically post the descriptions, images, and video you created to multiple social networks and web pages. For example, search Facebook for any local pages that allow people to post things they have for sale. You should do the same with Twitter and Google+. Post images of the house on Instagram and Pinterest. Post the video of your house on YouTube.

Once a house sells, you want to take down your online ads. Taking down your video tour on YouTube is also a good idea. Otherwise, people may get frustrated if they check several ads only to discover the house has already been sold.

With every social network posting, you should include links back to your website or the base website where your sales information is posted. In addition to including links back to your website, you should include contact information with every posting. You can't assume people will follow your links.

Encourage your friends and family to like and share your posts. Although they may not be personally interested, every time they like or share the post, all of their social contacts will see the post. The more the information is shared, the better your chances will be to reach the people actually looking to buy.

Virtual Staging

Another thing you can do is offer virtual staging. There are a couple of ways you can go about this. First, you can stage the house prior to taking pictures, so when people look online, it will be exactly what they see if they visit the house. Another thing you can do is create an interactive floor plan. This will allow users to see how furniture can be arranged in the space. If they have the measurements for their furniture, they can make sure it will fit in various rooms, as well as through the doorway or up the stairs. Virtual staging can increase the likelihood that searchers will visit the actual house.

Creating Marketing Material

If you are not working with a realtor, you will need to create your own marketing material. Even if you are working with a realtor, you may want to be involved in the creation of marketing material to ensure it is done to your standards. It requires only a brief search online to find humorous marketing failures committed by realtors. Additionally, understanding the type of marketing materials you need and the standard you want them to be at will help you to know quickly if the realtor is not doing a great job.

Fliers

Fliers are ideal for marketing because they can be posted in places where potential buyers may see them, they can be included in information boxes, and they can be passed out at showings, so potential buyers remember which houses they saw and liked. Fliers should include photos of the house and essential information like the address, asking price, number of bedrooms and bathrooms, and any other information that may give the house an advantage over other houses in the area.

Photos

You need high-quality photos of the interior and exterior of the house to include with all marketing material. The photos should not be taken until the house is renovated, cleaned, and ready to sell. Take a minute to search online for bad realtor photos, you will find dozens of examples of what not to do: bad pictures, bad angles, fuzzy images, etc. These images need to visually sell the house. If prospective buyers aren't impressed by the images, they aren't going to waste their time going to see the house in person.

Video

Do a walk-through of the house with your camera and create a video tour. People who are researching houses online like to get as much information as they can before actually making an appointment to see a house. A video tour will help them decide if they are interested, which will save you the time and energy of working with people who aren't really potential buyers.

Video tours will be highly informative and helpful for prospective buyers, but they will also help you attract more attention through search engines when people are searching for houses in your area.

When creating the video, be sure to show the entire house. Walk slowly and be careful not to rock or shake the camera too much; you don't want to make viewers sick. Speak slowly and clearly while narrating the tour. You can choose to have voice-over narration, or you can have someone in the video actually talking and pointing out different features while you film.

Finally, have the video edited. Simply taking a video yourself and then posting it online will make it look and feel like a home video. You want this to be professional looking. It isn't just selling your house; it is helping you to create your brand. If you do not know how to edit the video yourself, you can hire a freelancer to do it for you. It will be worth the money to have a professional-looking virtual tour video.

Selling Binders

A selling binder is essentially an overview of the property for the new homeowners. It includes proof of major items that have been recently replaced such as the roof, windows, furnace, or hot water heater. These are expensive and major repairs, so showing potential homeowners that these repairs have already been made adds value to the house.

The selling binder should also include any warranties that come with the repairs that have been made. The new owners will need all this information if they need work done in the near future. The selling binder should also include pictures of the house and the interior rooms. It should highlight the aspects of the house that increase its value compared to houses in the area.

You want to have the selling binder available for people to look through during open houses and showings. A great way to do this is to simply leave it out on the kitchen counter and let people know they are welcome to take a look. You should also bring the selling binder with you when you attend networking events. This way, if someone shows interest in the house, you can let them look through the selling binder.

Business Cards

You will need to create business cards with all of your contact information including your website, cell-phone number, and e-mail address. Whenever you are networking with other property investors, you can give them a card. When you hear someone talking about buying a house, you can give him a card. You can have friends and family pass your cards along to people they know are interested in buying a house. Let everyone know they should watch your website to see the houses you have available.

Open Houses and Showings

Open houses and showings are opportunities for potential buyers to tour the house, ask questions, and decide if they are interested. The open house is like the big production you've been carefully planning for. You want the house to look its best, and you want the open house to be well-advertised so a lot of people show up. Having a large number of people come to the open house will increase your networking opportunities and word-of-mouth advertising, and it will promote the house in the minds of those that attend. They will see how many other people appear to be interested in the house, and that will increase the pressure to make an offer quickly.

Don't feel like you have to go over the top during an open house. While a cheese tray and bottled water is nice to be able to offer people, you don't need to have a buffet of snacks available.

Preparing for an Open House or Showing

Before each open house or showing, you should go through the house quickly and look for any messes that may have been missed or left behind by mistake. Have a trash bag, a roll of paper towels, and a bottle of all purpose cleaner with you, just in case. Even if it is something as little as a dusty sink, you can quickly clean it up.

You also want to make sure there are high wattage light bulbs in every light fixture and that all the lights are turned on when the prospective buyers get there. Lighting up a room can make it look larger, cleaner, and more inviting. Finally, you want to make sure all the windows are clean and clear. Clean windows will allow more natural light into the house, but they also make the house appear more appealing. Dirty windows are easy to notice.

Post-Open House Evaluation

After each open house, it is good to take some time to consider some of the feedback you received from the visitors. Was there something a majority of the people complained about? If so, is it something you could quickly and easily fix? Is there something a majority of the people liked that you could promote at your next open house or showing?

Developing a Practical Strategy

With so many marketing strategies at your disposal, it is best to create a practical marketing strategy that you will follow utilizing both online and offline marketing tactics. Creating an actual plan will ensure that everything is done effectively and appropriately. Going into a marketing campaign without a plan will result in things being missed, as well as overall stress and frustration. The easiest way to make sure everything is completed and without stress is to plan everything out in advance. This is not a situation where "winging it" will be effective. It is important to remember that every day you are in possession of the house, it is costing you money. The goal is to sell it and sell it fast.

Creating a Marketing Calendar

A significant part of your marketing strategy will be creating a marketing calendar. This will include the dates that ads will be in the newspaper and published online. It will also include the deadlines for newspaper and other outlets to ensure the information is published on the days you want it to be public. Your calendar should include when and where you will be getting the fliers printed and yard signs prepared. Every marketing activity you partake in should be scheduled, so you don't miss deadlines.

Your marketing calendar for each house can be part of your greater editorial calendar, which will include when you will add new posts to your blog and what topics they will cover. It is best to use one calendar for all your business needs to avoid things being overlooked.

Delegating Marketing Tasks

If you are working with a realtor, she will be able to handle a great deal of the marketing tasks; that is her job. Additionally, the fliers and signs can come from the realtor, so these are two less tasks you will need to worry about. Let your realtor know what tasks you will accomplish and when you will accomplish them. For example, your realtor will be able to get your house listed on realty websites and added to the MLS. While she is handling that, you may be able to help by listing the property, videos, and images on your blog or website, your social networks, and other online resources you can work with.

If you aren't working with a realtor, you will need to assume the tasks a realtor would normally accomplish. There is a lot to be done, so if you have a business partner or assistant, it is a good idea to divide up the tasks. You focus on the tasks you are best at, and delegate the tasks that someone else can accomplish faster and more effectively. If you are delegating work to an assistant, you can also include busy work on his to-do list. For example, if you create the marketing fliers, your assistant can make sure they get printed. If you create the newspaper ad, your assistant can get it to the newspaper before the publishing deadline. When delegating tasks, do so in an effective manner. Don't just randomly split the to-do list in half and start working.

CHAPTER 11:

HOW TO SELL A HOUSE FOR THE MOST MONEY

S elling a house is one of the most important parts of real estate investing. There are many factors to consider when selling a house: the repairs that are needed, the time of year, and whether or not to use an agent.

What repairs are needed?

The condition of the house is critical to its salability. Seasoned investors and those experienced in real estate can see the potential in houses that need repairs. However, many first-time or move-up buyers have a hard time picturing a house if it needs work or does not show well. During showings, I have hosted as an agent, I learned that some buyers let paint color or furniture persuade them whether to buy a house or not.

The repairs you make are extremely important. The number and type of repairs will vary depending on market conditions and the house price. Usually, the more expensive the house, the more repairs and updates you should to do. The best way to figure out how many upgrades are needed is to look at your competition. View other houses that are for sale in the neighborhood. What types of flooring do they have? Do they have updated cabinets? How nice is the landscaping? And, how quickly are they selling?

Will staging help sell a house?

Staging can mean many things to many people. It can mean spending thousands of dollars to rent furniture for a vacant house, or it can mean cleaning and organizing an occupied house. When we sell a house, we do not stage. We sell many houses, and to be honest, one of the reasons we do not stage is we do not have the time. I know many investors who swear by staging and feel it brings them much more money. I think staging can create a very positive effect if done correctly. You cannot throw a table and two chairs in the living room and call it staged. To stage a house properly, each room needs to have at least the bare minimum of furniture that someone would want. Staging should show potential buyers what the house would feel like if they lived there. Personally, I like how big a house feels when it is completely vacant and has brand new paint and carpet.

I think staging is very important if people are living in a house. People tend to collect furniture and personal items over the years that clutter a house. The key to staging an occupied house is to de-clutter and de-personalize it as much as possible. When buyers look at a house, you want them to look at features, not personal pictures. You want them to picture themselves, not someone else, living there. When de-cluttering, it is best to remove all non-essential furniture and most decorations. You want the house to feel as large as possible, and the fewer items in the house, the larger it feels. When you sell, make sure the furniture is not too big for the rooms. Nothing makes a house feel smaller than a king-size bed in a small bedroom.

How important is the asking price?

When you sell a house, the thing that will attract buyers more than anything else is the price. When buyers and real estate agents search the MLS, they sort out potential properties based on price. I am always looking for low-priced deals that I can profit from, either as a rental or a fix and flip. Many buyers want to live in a specific neighborhood or in a particular area for a certain price. If you price your house higher than all the others in the neighborhood, it can be very difficult to sell. Most buyers have expectations for what certain areas cost, and if a house costs significantly more than that expectation, many buyers may never consider or view the property. You may also run into an appraisal issue, which I will talk about shortly.

Different types of markets will change how you sell. In a seller's market, there is much more flexibility concerning asking price and the repairs that are needed. I will actually price houses a little highly in a seller's market because there is very little competition. In a seller's market, many buyers are looking, but there are only a few houses for sale. Even if I price a house slightly high, buyers will still look at it. They may offer me less than I am asking but still make an offer. In a seller's market, I can sometimes make fewer repairs as well because I do not have five or ten other houses with which to compete.

In a buyer's market, everything changes. I price houses slightly below what I think market value is. I do this because I do not want to be caught chasing a declining market. When chasing a declining market, you may try to lower your price to get buyers, but you cannot lower it enough to catch falling prices. The house then stays on the market three months or more and becomes stigmatized. Whenever a house is on the market for an extended period, buyers automatically think something is wrong with it. Even if the price is great and the house is perfect, buyers will think there must be some reason no one else has bought it.

One of the biggest mistakes I see flippers make during the sale is pricing a house too highly. Even though I price mine a little highly now, it's because we're in a seller's market and I am very experienced. If you are just starting, be conservative and do not get greedy. Price the house where you know it will sell so you can get your money out quickly and buy something else.

How quickly do you need to sell a house?

If you want to sell the house you live in, the time it takes to make repairs or get the house perfect for marketing does not matter as much. The owner-occupant uses and lives in the home while it is being repaired. If you are an investor or have already moved out, you pay carrying costs while the house sits vacant. Most likely, you have a loan that you pay interest on along with utilities, insurance, and opportunity cost. Opportunity cost is the loss of potential profit on a new deal that you could have earned if your money had not been tied up. It can cost $50, $100, or more per day to carry a vacant house with a loan on it. Trying to squeak out a few thousand dollars on a house that is priced too high may instead cost you thousands.

Repairs will also cause delays that lead to additional carrying costs. When deciding whether to make minor or major repairs, make sure you figure the extra carrying costs involved in making those repairs.

Should you use an agent?

Real estate agents are expensive, but they are worth it. I may be biased, but there are only a few special instances where I would try to sell a house without an agent. It will almost always save you money and time. There will be much more on why you should use an agent later.

What is the best time of year to sell?

The time of year can affect how you sell a house. If you have a choice, it may be best to sell during spring or summer.

- Spring: Spring may be the best time of the year to sell. In the spring, people are outside enjoying the nice weather and the days are getting longer. Many people must work until five and cannot view houses until after work. During the winter, it is dark after work, making it much more difficult to view properties.

- Summer: Summer is a great time to sell. The weather is warm, the days are long, and many people have more free time. Many buyers also want to be settled into their house before school begins and all other fall activities start.

- Fall: Fall is a decent time to sell, but it is a risky time as well. Between the start of school, fall activities, and sports, people are very busy. Halloween and Thanksgiving also get in the way of house searches.

- Winter: Winter is the toughest time of year to sell. The holidays and cold weather tend to slow down the housing market. I happen to find many great deals in the winter because other buyers are preoccupied with the holidays. The days are very short and do not allow much viewing time.

I am not saying you should never sell a house in the winter or fall, but it is usually easier to sell in the spring or summer. We sell houses all year, and if you do everything else right, you can sell anytime. When I flip houses, I concentrate on buying the houses, repairing them quickly, and selling them. I am not concerned at all about the time of year. If you happen to live in an area with a highly cyclical market, it may be worth it to consider when you will be selling your fix and flip.

There are also some markets where everything I just said means nothing. In Florida, the best time to sell may be in the winter. There are more people in the area and the weather is much more pleasant.

Can appraisals affect the selling price?

We run into appraisal issues all the time, especially in an appreciating market. Appraisers must use sold comps when they determine value. In an appreciating market, it can be tough to find enough sold comps to justify rising prices. When you are deciding how many repairs to do, look at the sold comps in the neighborhood and make sure the sold comps support a higher value. If your house is going to be nicer and more expensive than everything else in the neighborhood, you may run into an appraisal issue.

If a house does not appraise for the contract price, buyers must base their loan value on the appraisal value. Many times, buyers do not have extra cash, and the only solution to a low appraisal is to find a new buyer or lower the price. If an FHA appraisal has been done, the appraisal stays with the house for four months, and any new FHA buyers must use that appraisal.

I often run into appraisal issues on my flips because I repair them and they sell at the top of the market. The more expensive a house compared to other houses in the neighborhood, the more likely it is that you will have an appraisal issue. If you are planning to renovate a house to try to get the highest price you can, make sure you are not overpricing it for the neighborhood. Not only will it be hard to get buyers to view it, but it also may not appraise for your contract price.

How does the 90-day flip rule affect the selling process?

There used to be a 90-day flip rule on FHA loans for buyers. The rule would not allow lenders to loan on properties that had sold within the last 90 days. Even though that rule was suspended, many lenders still abide by it. Some lenders allow a second appraisal within 90 days of the sale to verify value; some make everyone wait 90 days; and others do not pay attention to the rule at all. Foreclosures that a bank repurchases are exempt from this rule. If you are going to flip a house and plan to sell it within 90 days of the purchase date, be aware that you may run into a problem with the 90-day flip rule.

CHAPTER 12:

THE MAKINGS OF A FLOP - COMMON MISTAKES TO AVOID

All the choices you make between deciding to flip a house and finally making a sale (or enacting any other exit strategy) will determine the profitability of your venture. If you make any mistakes that you fail to address along the way, then it's possible that you might come to a loss.

That said, it's ideal that you maintain awareness of the things that could turn your flip into a flop. This way, you can anticipate them and adjust your actions and responses to mitigate the problems that could arise later on as a result.

Choosing the Wrong House

It was stated in one of the earlier chapters that your choice of property will be the foundation of your success. And that will always hold true in the business of flipping. Failing to make the right considerations when choosing a home can turn your venture into a money hungry nightmare, sapping you of time and resources, and causing you to incur a loss when all is said and done.

Unfortunately, it can be hard to detect a "bad" house right off the bat, especially if you're not experienced enough. Lots of properties look like great choices, and you might get a strong enough gleam in your eye to jump the gun and make the purchase because it looked like a good pick.

But there's more to choosing a house than just considering appearances. There's the issue of location, age, and specifications. Is it accessible? Was it built before 1978? Does it compete with other houses for sale in the area in terms of size and capacity?

Before you make a decision, try to imagine yourself living in that house. What might have seemed like an ideal place in the neighborhood might actually be inaccessible to main roads. What might have seemed like a great layout might be an interior design nightmare. What might have seemed like a cozy blueprint might actually be subpar compared to more spacious choices in the area.

Ignoring the Neighbors

Every flipper loves the satisfaction of working with a shabby shack and turning into a beautiful single-family unit for a budding couple expecting their first baby. But be careful - some of the ugliest houses in the neighborhood might be flanked by equally ugly properties.

Don't let tunnel vision drive you to make a decision that might be difficult to rectify later on. Make sure you check the neighbors too to make sure your house is in a place that people would want to pay good money to be. If the next-door properties look like run-down danger zones, then it might not be worth it.

Paying Too Much

So you found a great property in an ideal location - and you're really sure about this one! Not only does it compete with other houses for sale in the area in terms of size, it comes at a really reasonable price, too. It was probably made for you - don't you think?

You take out a loan and buy that house without making negotiations. You like it too much to lose your shot! So now it's yours and you go through with renovations. Everything proceeds without a hitch, and you're happy to put your property on the market in just 4 months' time.

But now that you crunch the numbers - uh oh. It seems something's just not adding up. What happened? Why does your profit look like your 12th grade bank account? You trace back the issue and find the root cause - you paid too much for the house at the start.

This is one of the most common problems that first-time flippers run into. Because most are convinced that those primary computations are purely speculative, they feel that they're unnecessary. However, just because they're inaccurate, doesn't mean they can't be used to guide those first few steps into making an investment.

Knowing how much you stand to make before you purchase a property is an important aspect of flipping. If you do away with the numbers at any given point throughout the process, you run the risk of reducing your profit and potentially even incurring a loss.

Before you make a purchase, make sure you've got your computations in check. Consider how much other houses in the area are selling for and use that as an estimate of your ARV. Then consider the cost of renovation, and weigh all the numbers together. The 70% Rule would be a very nifty tool to use at this point in time.

Poor Renovation Choices

When you renovate your home, you want to do everything just right. Bring it up to standards, make it compete with other properties for sale, but don't overdo it so that it sticks out like a sore thumb amidst the competition. Use other houses as a gauge and always check back on what those properties offer if you feel unsure of what you're doing.

If you skimp out on renovations and make insufficient changes, your property will end up looking like an outdated option compared to the others around it. This is of course, on top of the potential functional problems that it might have.

If you pay for too many renovations, your property will end up much too expensive compared to others, making it difficult to lock in a buyer especially because they have more reasonably priced choices in the same area.

Before starting any sort of repair or change, always, always, always make it a point to check what the others offer. Use their homes as a guiding light and don't step beyond what they offer even if it doesn't necessarily appeal to your own preference. This is about meeting the buyers' expectations, not satisfying your own personal renovation preferences.

Overlooking Permits and Fees

There's a lot more to getting renovations done than just buying materials and contacting a contractor. There are permits, fees, and other papers that you need to secure in order to get started, and they're not always that easy to acquire. Sometimes, it could take weeks before a municipality can give you the go signal, and that can easily eat away at your timetable.

Before you even start to purchase any possible investments, familiarize yourself with the process of renovation. Map out the time it takes to get certain permits, and figure out how much extra you might need to have in order to cover all the costs as they come.

Miscalculating Holding Fees

A commonly overlooked expense is the holding or carrying fee. These charges will continue to run as long as you haven't found a buyer for your home yet. So be sure you have some sort of fund to pay them off with if you're anticipating that the sale might take a while.

There are lots of fix n' flip investors who lose all their profit on holding fees, especially when they don't get to make a sale as soon as they want to. This can easily eat away at your own savings and bank account, so be careful. Factor them into your budget beforehand and make sure you have just enough to fund them before they get out of hand.

Using Standard Smartphones for Pictures

Tons of ads posted online, and not a single inquiry. What gives? Before you blame the internet, consider this - maybe your ads don't look appealing enough. Most newbies tend to think that it doesn't really matter. A good looking, decently located property will sell itself, right? Wrong. In any case, you are responsible for selling your property, and that entails taking the time when it comes to developing your advertisement.

Remember that 50% of buyers will start with the web when in search of a home to purchase. So make the most of these platforms so they work in your favor. Expert flippers will even hire a professional photographer to compose shots and perform post-process to generate high-quality images that just rake in new leads. Of course, we might not all have that kind of budget, but it does pay to be particular with your listings.

If you can't hire a professional photographer, at least try to learn a few tricks to be able to capture high-quality photos. These can change the way your ads perform and may even bring a serious buyer to your doorstep sooner rather than later.

Not Posting Enough

If you were hoping to gain traction with that one Facebook post you published on your profile, you've got another thing - or absolutely nothing - coming. The purpose of online posting is extending your reach to people you wouldn't be able to reach any other way. There are people in neighboring states or even other countries who are looking to move in where your property is located - how can they find out about your house if you're not extending your visibility?

You can't just post once on Facebook or Zillow and be done with it. There's a benefit to continuously updating your listings. Newer listings often get indexed first, and that gives you the advantage of being seen before any other choices on a list.

So aside from posting on real estate websites, consider joining Facebook groups where you might find interested buyers. On top of that, it's also vital that you post regularly even if that means posting the same ads over and over again.

You never know who might be scanning those search results now - you might reach a completely new batch of viewers if you post today compared to those that you reached yesterday.

It also helps to reword your listings as you post them. You'll notice that words like "NEWLY RENOVATED" and "SPACIOUS" might receive more attention than headlines that use bland words. Keep it interesting and write in a way that would encourage others to click your link and learn more about your post.

Fitting Everything Into an Unreasonable Timetable

There's beauty in achieving a quick flip, but there's no need to force it. While we all want to be able to make a sale as soon as possible, there's something to be gained out of taking your time where it's necessary.

Buyers these days are exceptionally meticulous, and they'll even call in experts to tell them what they don't know. So if you're trying to hide a few flaws in your home, hoping that they go unnoticed, you should know that they will definitely be seen.

Instead of trying to force a timetable that's just too short, allot time where you feel it's necessary. Don't pressure your contractors to get the job done faster, but try to make sure that they're not taking more time than they need.

Make sure all of the changes that need to be done are completed properly and appropriately. This way, you can snag a sale sooner instead of having to go back and forth trying to fix things you thought you could skip.

Pushing Plan A

We all love a guy (or gal!) who can stand her ground. But there is a time when it becomes impractical and just downright, well - stupid. A major concept you need to accept is that not all flips will go your way. Some will exceed your expectations and work out better than you thought, and others will completely drive you insane, wishing you had stuck to your day job instead.

Acknowledging that plans change even when you don't want them to will make it easier for you to switch to plan B when things start to go downhill. But if you choose to believe in your primary plan, if you think it can still work out and you just need a little more faith even if all the signs are telling you to disengage, then we've got a problem.

There's a lot to lose if your flip starts turning into a flop, and you need to be ready to switch gears when that happens. Remove your emotions from the situation and try to see things objectively. Emotional attachment to a venture is the leading cause of loss.

Paying Full for Materials

There are tons of budget-friendly options out there that can help you maximize your resources when buying supplies for the renovations. So don't shell out double the cost on materials that are of similar quality. Remember, in a lot of ways, retail is mostly about brands. Certain brands cost more than others, despite being exactly the same.

Exercise your shopping muscle when looking for discounted construction materials and always ask for alternatives to anything you find on the shelves. The odds are, those store clerks probably have something stored in the back that meets your needs without having to cost too much.

You might also want to check your credit cards for possibly rebates and rewards. Buying all of your supplies using these cards can give you access to exclusive offers and discounts that might not help with the construction per se, but still give you better value for the money you spend.

Avoiding the Experts

Sure, hiring a few extra professionals to help you out with your cause might cost you more now, but if you're really unsure how to get things done, then is there really any other choice? As an investor, there's something to gain out of being humble and practical enough to seek help when you know you're at a loss.

If you feel like you're having trouble figuring out the design for your house, call in an architect. If you can't DIY anything for the project, have the contractors do everything. If you're worried you might not be able to find a suitable buyer in time, ask a realtor to help you out.

Yes, it will cost you money to hire these people and ask them for their expertise. But at the end of the day, you can feel confident that you didn't skimp out on your project and that you have someone who knows what they're doing with your property. This doesn't only secure its ARV, but also helps ascertain that you won't have to wait for a buyer too long after making a listing.

Underestimating Staging

This is a good looking house, I don't really need to do a lot with it. For some people, staging can be fun and interesting. But for others (mostly men), it can be a tedious chore. No one wants to spend their time decorating a space that's not even theirs. Besides, if a house is good enough, it will pretty much sell itself.

Unfortunately, there's a lot to gain out of staging and sellers who don't leverage its inherent benefits run the risk of losing prospects and having their property sit on the market for way too long.

The purpose of staging is to paint a picture for your buyers. This is what you can do with this property. This could be how you live. It makes sense of a space and puts context. It makes it easier to see how your own life can unfold in a place you've never seen before. It taps into emotions - a powerful driving force in the realm of purchasing property.

If you don't want to go through the challenge of staging a house, try hiring someone to do it for you. There are countless home stagers out there who charge a minimal fee to help you dress your house up and sell it to prospects. In some cases, your real estate agent might already be offering that service for the amount that you pay them. Make sure to ask about it before you stage to find out how they can be of assistance.

Thinking It's a One-Man Job

While you might be the brains of this outfit, you need to recognize the indispensable role of the other people who are a part of your team. Your contractors, your agents, architects, and everyone else involved in the process is as much a part of the project as you are. So don't think you can do it all on your own.

A lot of times, newbies feel the need to micromanage their projects, assuming it's the best way to meet their goals and make a profit. But when it comes right down to it, these professionals probably know more about the industry than you do. So don't try to dictate how they should get their job done.

Trust the people you have on your team, learn from them, and make sure they get to provide their opinion especially if they're giving one on a topic that they're particularly knowledgeable about. After all, that's what you hired them for in the first place, right?

Spitballing the ARV

There are a lot of ways you can come up with the figures to represent your ARV. For instance, you can visit the neighborhood and check out the prices for other houses for sale. You can go online and see how much the houses in the area are selling for in general. You can base it off of the purchase price you got your property for, and see how all the cost of renovations can factor in to give you an idea of how much you can sell it for once it's all done.

While these all give you some idea as to the ARV of your property, none of those numbers can be certain. So it's always best to seek out a real estate agent who can help you develop a more accurate idea of what you can expect when you make a sale. The importance of knowing your ARV is that it can guide you as to the expense you can incur without eating up all your profit.

Don't make mistakes with those initial calculations, and if you can, find someone who can give you the most accurate estimations to help your project along the way to reasonable profit.

Doing Eraser Math

What a great piece of property! I wonder how I can make it fit my budget? If you find yourself having to ask that question in the first place, you might be better off looking elsewhere. Eraser math can be a deadly pit that can cause you to feel financially capable when you actually aren't.

For instance, some newbies will erase original anticipated ARVs and renovation fees in order to bump up their maximum purchase price. Sure, it might make your project seem like a financially sound opportunity on paper, but changing up the ARV in your logbook won't change it in real life.

Once you finally have your listing up, you'll find that it won't sell for your imaginary ARV because that's precisely what it was - an imaginary number you came up with just so you could get your hands on a property you really liked.

Stick to the numbers and trust the computations. Don't try to bend or flex the calculations just to make ends meet - you'll be thankful for it.

Making Your Savings a Part of the Equation

We've all heard those stories - people flipping houses without having a dime to their name. Once you do start flipping though, you'll realize the harsh reality that pocket money is something you have to have if you want to rehab properties.

While a lot of your expenses will be funded by a financing entity or a loan, you need to know that you will spend some of your money on the venture. Unexpected fees, repairs, permits, and other unforeseen charges can require you to pay for certain values out of your own pockets - and that's okay.

What's important is making sure you set limits. Unless you plan to fund everything from your own personal accounts, it's imperative that you list down all the times you paid for something with your own money. This helps make it easier to understand where profit ends and losses begin.

Failing to factor in the money you spent from your own savings could make it hard to detect whether you've made a profit at all. For instance, some flippers think they made this much when in fact, they only really made a fraction because they forgot to list down the times they spent on things from their own wallet.

On top of that, putting a limit on the amount you're willing to pay for yourself saves you from the danger of losing everything you have to your project. Of course, we all want to see our hard work come up with something good, but if it means shelling out everything you have, then you might want to look into a plan B.

Forgetting the Buyers

It's easy to get carried away when you're dealing with a renovation. You have color preferences, interior design inspiration, and lots of other concepts you want to try out to create a space that's uniquely you.

Unfortunately, developing a space that caters to your taste means you might end up forgetting what the buyers want to see. For the most part, people who are interested in purchasing a property want a space that looks clean, that's functional, and that can be easily adapted to their preferred interior design style.

If you incorporate too many factors that cater to your unique preferences, then it might be difficult for your buyers to see themselves in that space. So instead of letting your desire to design get the best of you, stick to the status quo. Follow what other houses for sale in the area have to offer. Don't stray too far. At the end of the day, plain vanilla sells.

Believing Too Strongly In Your Property

We all have the tendency to trust our own. It's just our natural disposition to feel proud of what's ours. So when you look at your property, you might be thinking, wow, this here's a real masterpiece.

While it's true that it might look like a real winner, you have to keep your expectations in line. Not everyone will see your property the same way because they weren't there when all the blood, sweat, and tears came pouring down. There will be low ballers and buyers who will look and scoff - it's all part of the process.

What you don't want is to let your belief in your property to dictate your decisions. If it feels like you're not getting the attention you deserve, or if you're struggling to make a sale, it might be time to bring down that selling price. While you might think your investment should be worth its weight in gold, the market probably doesn't and that's just the harsh reality.

Losing Sight of Time

First-time flippers often get caught up in the renovation process that they end up taking their sweet time. Sure, we all want to make the best out of what we have. But if that means shaving off significant amounts of time, then you should reconsider your strategy.

Losing sight of your timetable can make it very possible to exceed your designated time limit. If you reach your hard money loan due and you're still just wrapping up the repairs, then you've got yourself a problem.

Other than that, the time you spend rehabbing your property will dictate how much you'll have to pay in terms of holding fees. The longer you hold on to the house, the longer you extend your temporary ownership. In the long run, this could sap you of any profit and even cause a loss.

Establish a sound timetable before you start your project and make sure everyone on your team has a copy. Keep it somewhere visible and try to get updates from everyone to find out which part of the process they're currently working on. This should help keep everything in order and prevent your team from exceeding the allotted time.

Is this an all-inclusive list? Quite the contrary. There are a lot of other mistakes you could make - newbie or not. So it's important to read up and audit yourself throughout the entire process of the flip. The best way to avoid these issues to stay on top of operations and keep your eyes open in case of any potential problems.

There's no way to really eliminate risk 100% if you're flipping. And a lot of the decisions you make will rely on your foresight. Give yourself some time to learn and don't avoid the professionals - they're there to offer you knowledge and assistance. As you grow into your craft, you can start taking on more of the responsibilities to cut the cost without harming the outcomes of your endeavor.

CONCLUSION

I hope my book has provided relevant insight on how to set up your house flipping business and begin turning homes into greater profits than ever before. I have been flipping houses about 15 years and can recall helping my parents paint and sand as a young child. If you are new to the business of flipping houses, we hope you'll try some of these proven strategies and also share some new ones you pick up along the way.

The next step is to find a house to flip. Join some investor organizations and begin to develop relationships with other flippers. Enjoy all the benefits of shared marketing efforts, new renovation ideas, and money saving opportunities.

Finally, if you enjoyed this book, then I'd like to ask you for one more favor. Would you be kind enough to leave a review for this book wherever you purchased it? It would be greatly appreciated!